T0112997

PENGUIN BUSINESS

MARKETING TO MILLENNIALS

Vivek Iyyani is a globally recognized leadership expert and keynote speaker helping organizations and leaders work better together in the new normal. Vivek has spoken, worldwide, to organizations and enterprises from Fortune 500 companies to associations and government institutions. He is the founder and CEO of Millennial Minds—a company that has helped leaders and teams leverage twenty-first-century collaboration skills globally. He has been invited to many international media outlets to share his opinions as a thought leader on the millennial generation. Some of his recent features include Channel NewsAsia, Money FM, Straits Times, SME Entrepreneur Magazine, CEO Magazine, and National Integration Council (Singapore Prime Minister's Office). He has authored three other books titled *Empowering Millennials*, *Engaging Millennials*, and *The Millennial Leader*. Learn more at https://www.vivekiyyani.com and follow him at @vivekiyyani on LinkedIn, Facebook, Instagram, TikTok and Twitter.

Scan QR code to get your bonus resources

ADVANCE PRAISE

'The book is an essential guide for every marketer aiming to understand and successfully cater to the millennial generation. As a digital marketing agency owner, I found the book rich with practical insights and transformative strategies for crafting meaningful connections in the digital era. The book has transformed the way we approach and engage with the most influential demographic in today's marketplace.'
—Razy Shah, CEO, 2Stallions Digital Marketing Agency

'Today, digital natives are in control and it's harder than ever to win their attention. Vivek's books illuminates an insightful roadmap on how to transform your marketing to influence change in buying behaviours, grow revenues and accelerate growth.'
—Maneesh Sah, Author of *The New Marketer*

'Without a doubt, *Marketing to Millennials* is a must-read. This book has the power to reshape the marketing landscape, making it an indispensable asset for anyone seeking to thrive in today's ever-evolving digital era. Vivek's passion for empowering others shines through every chapter, inspiring readers to push boundaries, challenge conventions, and embrace innovation in their marketing strategies.'
—Debapriya (Priya), CEO, Social Connection

ALSO BY VIVEK IYYANI

Engaging Millennials: 7 Fundamentals to Recruit, Reward & Retain the Largest Generation in the Workforce, Penguin Random House SEA, 2021
The Millennial Leader: Working across Generations in the New Normal, Penguin Random House SEA, 2022

Marketing to Millennials

How to Get the Digital Natives Lining Up to Do Business with You

Vivek Iyyani

BUSINESS
An imprint of Penguin Random House

PENGUIN BUSINESS

USA | Canada | UK | Ireland | Australia
New Zealand | India | South Africa | China | Southeast Asia

Penguin Business is part of the Penguin Random House group of companies
whose addresses can be found at global.penguinrandomhouse.com

Published by Penguin Random House SEA Pte Ltd
9, Changi South Street 3, Level 08-01,
Singapore 486361

First published in Penguin Business by Penguin Random House SEA 2023

Copyright © Vivek Iyyani 2023

All rights reserved

10 9 8 7 6 5 4 3 2 1

The views and opinions expressed in this book are the author's own and the
facts are as reported by him which have been verified to the extent possible,
and the publishers are not in any way liable for the same.

ISBN 9789814914147

Typeset in Adobe Garamond Pro by MAP Systems, Bengaluru, India

This book is sold subject to the condition that it shall not, by way of trade
or otherwise, be lent, resold, hired out, or otherwise circulated without the
publisher's prior consent in any form of binding or cover other than that in
which it is published and without a similar condition including this
condition being imposed on the subsequent purchaser.

www.penguin.sg

To my lovely wife and soulmate, Sushmitha

Contents

Foreword

In today's digital landscape, understanding and engaging with the Millennial and Gen Z generations can be a challenge. To help navigate this complexity, *Marketing to Millennials: How to get the digital natives lining up to do business with you* offers valuable insights.

Authored by Vivek Iyyani, a true visionary and expert in the field, this book provides a deep understanding of the unique mindset, aspirations, and behaviours of Millennials and Gen Zs. It explores their desire for authenticity, personalization, and social responsibility.

The book goes beyond understanding and equips readers with practical techniques for capturing attention and building lasting relationships. It covers strategies like leveraging social media, influencer marketing, and storytelling to connect with the millennial audience. Through real-world case studies and success stories, readers gain inspiration and actionable wisdom. The book empowers marketers to challenge conventional wisdom and embrace new approaches to engage the millennial audience.

Marketing to Millennials offers a blueprint for success, shaping the future of businesses seeking to tap into the millennial mindset. It's a valuable resource for those aiming to adapt and thrive in the digital marketplace.

Embark on this enlightening journey and unleash the potential of the millennial generation with the guidance provided in *Marketing to Millennials*. It's time to adapt and conquer the challenges of marketing to millennials and elevate your business to new heights.

—Dipashree Das
Head of Partner Marketing for APAC & ANZ @ Amazon

How to Extract the Most Value
out of this Book

When I was asked by my publisher to write this book, the biggest thought that kept reappearing in my mind was: Why would anyone want to read a book specifically about how to market to Millennials? What makes them so special that we need to have a specific strategy just for them? At the end of the day, aren't we all humans? As a reader, I'm sure you've probably had that thought cross your mind as well. As I went deeper into the research, it became clear that there are age-based, generational trends that are very useful for the marketer. Our culture is changing very rapidly, and in many ways, people function differently today than they used to do a generation ago.

According to Pew Research Center, 74 per cent of Millennials are more likely to believe that technology makes life easier, compared to 69 per cent of Gen Xers and 60 per cent of Baby Boomers. Younger generations are more likely to believe that their lives and their jobs will get easier with technology. This is becoming a trend, and trends are useful for marketers to take note of. Market researchers have had a long history of segmenting the population into broad categories composed of individuals with common interests and priorities. They use this information to create a marketing strategy and target them. That's when it hit me:

Marketers will waste money if their target market is too broad.

In this game of marketing, the narrower you focus, the higher your returns are. In order to make the most out of this book, you must truly believe this, and be willing to experiment and step out of your comfort zone based on this principle. This is the mindset that is required to extract the most value out of this book. With Millennials being online all day, marketers need to get creative to get their brand noticed above all the noise from intrusive ads, pop-ups, notifications, tweets, and messages. To attract Millennials, marketers need their messages to rise above the noise. With social networks and technological advances like artificial intelligence, it is possible to go from broad audiences into narrower audiences. The data we collect online can make it even easier for marketers to reach this group that spends a good amount of their time on social media. You can find out their hobbies, friends, job interests, pets, volunteer work, and vacation plans just from their social media profiles. Everything, from technological trends to financial trends, to sociological trends, has influenced the mindset that Millennials have today. Lost in the digital, artificially intelligent, volatile, uncertain, complex and ambiguous (VUCA) world of the Fourth Industrial Revolution, it isn't hard to get overwhelmed and paralyzed by the complexity of modern life.

As you delve into the pages of this book, I urge you to find a cozy and comfortable spot to enjoy the journey of introspection that awaits you. Picture a warm, inviting atmosphere—perhaps a plush couch, a cup of hot cocoa, fragrant candles, and soothing melodies. I humbly implore you to approach this reading experience with an open mind and heart, and to let your guard down in order to fully absorb the innovative concepts and ideas presented within.

To make the most of your reading experience, I suggest keeping a journal nearby. Each chapter has been thoughtfully crafted to challenge outdated methods and encourage the adoption of new perspectives. Each chapter also contains a set of questions designed to prompt self-reflection on your personal journey as a marketer. It is through this introspection that you will gain invaluable insights. The more effort you invest in these reflections, the more profound your realizations will become. I even recommend revisiting each chapter, as this allows for greater clarity of the concepts discussed and a chance to uncover ideas that may have been missed initially. Reading provides knowledge, but the act of writing allows for a deeper understanding of the insights presented. Additionally, I have provided a variety of worksheets and exercises to complement the book, which can be accessed at www.vivekiyyani.com/free.

Who this book is for (and not for)

This book is for the individual who wants to learn how to market to Millennials better. In my conversations with many people, I've noticed that many tend to refer to young people as Millennials. It has become a synonym for the word 'youth'. Although if you look into it closely, the oldest Millennials have crossed forty. Simply put, I'm including Gen Zs into this bracket and I'll explain why in detail in the first chapter. So long story short, I'm writing this book for the marketers and executives at small, medium, and large companies who want to specifically target the younger generation. In order to get their attention, marketers need to talk to them, not at them. There's a subtle difference that is missed by many, and this book reveals it fully. This book is also for small-business owners and entrepreneurs with fresh, innovative ideas. It is for the solopreneurs as well, who wear many hats where their livelihoods depend on their marketing skills i.e. the coaches, consultants, accountants, doctors, lawyers, and therapists, who are progressive enough to change the way they market themselves. This book is also relevant to leaders in the government and non-profit organizations, who need to build their online presence and influence to drive positive change in the world. Many non-profits often struggle with the same challenges of today's businesses. This book is also for students and teachers of business, who want to look into newer ways of marketing and experimenting with it.

So, who is this book not for?

This book is not for everyone. It's not for the data scientists who want to go through files of research. I share lots of stories to bring my points across, but it's not something that is proven by science. Sometimes we rely too much on science to validate concepts that are already working in the real world, and that hurts business people who need actionable steps to move the needle. Research in laboratories hardly reflects the realities of the real world. This book is not for the individual who wants the latest, most updated information, because it's a book, not a blog post that can be updated as and when something new comes up. Last but not least, it's not for those who hate Millennials or Gen Zs, because if you hate them, well, it's going to be hard to influence them, let alone get them to buy from you.

Chapter 1

The 5G Marketer

On 17 July 2022, Jessica Lee, an Australian traveller, returned home from Singapore. Upon landing in Australia, she was slammed with an A$2,664 fine for having a half-eaten foot-long Subway sandwich she carried with her. She ate half of her sandwich, and saved the other half and brought it home to Perth. Her mistake?

She forgot to tick 'Chicken' and 'Lettuce' in her declaration form.

As a typical Millennial, Jessica pulled out her smartphone, and shared the incident on TikTok. A day later, Jessica is filming another video of herself unboxing a swag box from Subway, which included many goodies. It came with a card that said, 'To say thank you for eating fresh, we've uploaded a Sub card with A$2,664 just for you. We hope this covers all your chicken and lettuce needs.'

Lee's unboxing video on TikTok was later watched 1.1 million times within a day. This incident was picked up by many news channels over the world and became an internet sensation instantly. In marketing terms, Subway paid about $2,664 dollars to get over a million views. That's some pretty insane returns of investment. Here are some questions that come to mind:

- How was this possible?
- What conditions were needed to be aligned for this to happen?
- Was this pure luck, or carefully orchestrated strategy based on a deeper understanding of the young generation?

My guess is that, Subway was more than just lucky. Subway clearly had its means of social listening to catch wind of what happened. In this day and age, you cannot afford to be ignorant of social media trends and specifically be tuning in to posts that make your brand go viral. On top of that, speed is essential when it comes to social media. Imagine if the marketing team at Subway had to go through lots of red tape and multiple sign-offs to execute this strategy. It would have been a lost opportunity if bureaucracy was rampant. Moreover, this action is seen as being in line with their core values of 'family, teamwork, and opportunity'. They treated Jessica Lee, their customer, as their family, and worked together as a team to lift her spirits from the fine she received. Did Subway need to do this? Not at all. They didn't have to get involved just because a nineteen-year-old didn't do her due diligence. Yet, they chose to do something and leverage the opportunity to do good. That action reflects their values as an organization. Clearly, Subway knows what their values are and how to showcase them to this age group.

Now, would the same incident have made the news and gone viral in 1980, for example? Probably not, for a variety of reasons. Firstly, technology wasn't as developed to have the news spread as quickly. The computer and the internet were in their infancy stage and social media wasn't even a thing back then. The topics that made the news were strictly controlled by the people who distributed the news i.e. the newspapers, radio stations, and TV news shows. You probably agree with me, getting fined for carrying a Subway sandwich is hardly a newsworthy topic. And yet, it became viral because it created controversy. The video became a topic of who's right and who's wrong—which triggered the algorithm that fuelled this story. Would this topic have been seen as a controversial one back in 1980? Probably not. People had bigger things to worry about back then.

We have big changes in the marketing landscape, driven by huge technology transformation, tremendous advancement in data analytics, and changes in consumer behaviour driven by mobile and social media. Put together, these changes have flipped the switch on traditional marketing strategies. New technologies such as artificial intelligence, augmented reality, 5G connectivity, the Internet of Things, smart speakers, wearables, and blockchains are poised to disrupt marketing and transform consumer's lives.[1]

We live in a world of intense competition to generate new businesses, retain existing clientele and grow revenues in every industry. Every marketer is out and about to capture your audience's attention and not surprisingly, your customers are bombarded and overwhelmed by the marketing chaos we see today. With over 60,000,000,000 messages sent out on digital platforms each day, we have a crazy amount of information being placed in front of us daily. Seventy-nine per cent of smartphone owners check their device within fifteen minutes of waking up every morning. The urge to visit TikTok, Instagram, YouTube just for a few minutes that ends up in the never-ending doomscrolling behaviour for hours has become universal. It has become an urge that we all tend to feel throughout the day but we hardly notice it as it has become a habit. Our brains have started adjusting to the vast amount of content that needs to be processed than ever before. An average person spends about eleven hours a day interacting with digital media and scrolls through 300 feet of content. According to Brendan Kane, author of *Hook Point*, people use their phones 1,500 times a week and check their email inboxes about thirty times an hour.[2]

To make things even more complicated, you are now dealing with the Millennial consumers who happen to be the most aware, connected, and

---

[1] R. Rajamannar, *Quantum Marketing: Mastering the New Marketing Mindset for Tomorrow's Consumers.* (HarperCollins Leadership, 2021)

[2] B. Kane, B, *Hook Point: How to stand out in a 3-Second world.* (Independently published by the author, 2022).

sophisticated generation. Whenever they have issues with companies or with customer service reps or salespeople, they share those issues with the world through social media. I'm sure you've read some stories on social media yourself of companies that frustrate us to our wit's end. Millennials hold companies to high standards of products and service, and when those standards aren't met, they share. And they don't just share the bad. They also share the good business experiences that we have. For example, when there are good organizations out there listening to customers, responding to changing needs, and are passionate and grateful, we share about those too. Millennial consumers have the opportunity and responsibility to hold businesses accountable to high standards through social networks. It gives businesses the ability to receive direct and immediate feedback from their consumers.

According to entrepreneur Peter Diamandis, if you are holding a smartphone in your hands today, you have more access to information than the president of the United States did in the late 1990s. The smartphone gives this group the ability to make an impact through knowledge acquired by research or by sharing those messages that influence people and businesses.[3] Today, the number is between 4,000 to 10,000 ads per day. This means more and more people are tuning out ads that don't have any relevance to the consumer. According to Prezi, we are becoming more selective about what we devote our attention to. The inundation of platforms force marketers to compete harder than ever before because there's a lot of distraction. Don't believe me, just observe people in a public space. Chances are, you can spot them glued to their devices, be it their phone, tablet or laptop. Not only do you have competition for more content, you are competing with people who have better quality of content. You are literally fighting for limited time and attention as many messages get lost in the avalanche of distraction.

They wake up and go to sleep by looking at social media and the non-stop notifications showcase how easily they can get distracted (because other brands are out there vying for their attention). They use

---

[3] S. Carr, *How Many Ads Do We See a Day in 2023?* (Lunio. Retrieved 4 May 2023, from https://lunio.ai/blog/strategy/how-many-ads-do-we-see-a-day/)

ad-blocker on their sites so as to have an enhanced experience while browsing the web. Even their lingo is different, with words like salty, GOAT, receipts all having a different meaning altogether when they use it (salty isn't referring to the taste, GOAT isn't referring to the animal, and receipts are not about that piece of paper you get after a purchase).

Their work and purchasing preferences differ from the older generations and it can feel like a game of catch-up for many. Marketers trying to get the Millennial's buy-in need to understand the Millennial mindset. It's all about understanding their psyche and being able to invite them in to consider the solutions you provide to their problems. In order to do that, we need to go back to building a connection with this group on the medium that they are most comfortable with. Yes, you need to get 'down' to their level to get their attention and win their trust.

You no longer have customers alone. You need to have fans. It is vital to understand the Millennials and create an emotional bond. The world that the Millennials and Gen Zs have grown up in is starkly different from the world the Baby Boomers and Gen Xers did. The aim of this book is to explore the changes that have happened over the decades and to detail out how it has changed the way businesses acquire customers and brand loyalty. Often, this requires adjusting your brand and marketing strategy, product offerings, and marketing outreach to appeal to Millennials. As global connectivity continues to soar, generational shifts could come to play a more important role in setting behaviour than socioeconomic differences. Millennials are the digital natives, the multitaskers, progressives, and purpose-driven souls, who are highly aware of their capabilities and the power they wield. This book is going to show you how you can connect better with your younger customers so it becomes easy for them to buy from you. Young people have become a potent influence on people of all ages and incomes, as well as on the way those people consume and relate to brands. Businesses must rethink the way they deliver value to the consumer, rebalance scale, and mass production against personalization and most importantly, practice what they preach when they address marketing issues and work ethics.

Why I chose to write this book

'Everything in business is downstream from lead generation.'
—Daniel Priestley, CEO of Dent Global

For the uninitiated, 'lead generation' is the term used to describe the process of identifying and cultivating potential customers for a businesses' products and services. When you visit a website and they offer a freebie in exchange for your name and email address, that's lead generation. Similarly, when you sign up for the two-week trial at the gym and the salesperson hands you a form to fill in twenty contacts in your phone to 'qualify' for the free trial, that is also seen as lead generation. There are an infinite number of ways to generate leads, and yet, many businesses suffer from lack of leads. Many believe that without leads, it's difficult to run a business sustainably.

This quote above never made any sense to me when I had just started out my business. I didn't have any problems with lead generation—finding interested customers who are looking to buy something—based on the business I had embarked on with my friends right after graduation. While I was studying psychology in university, I was also working part-time as a youth coach in multiple organizations. It was on an hourly-wage basis and it was my personal training ground to get some experience. After failing my A Levels and going into a private university, I had pretty much decided for myself that no employer would want me and there was no way I would be given an internship. That was pretty much the moment I realized that I had a better chance at entrepreneurship than being an employee. Even though I was paid a mere $7/hour wage for my freelancing gigs back then, I enjoyed the work. I was so passionate about it that I volunteered to do more than was required of me. I gave feedback, took up leadership roles for different events, and learnt the ropes as a freelancer. Slowly, as I got more experience under my belt, I reached out to more companies with my profile and started understanding how the training industry for the school market worked. Some companies were really good, and some others were downright horrible. And it was during one of these school events (that was so horribly organized) that I thought to myself, 'Geez, I could do a better job than them!'

And that's exactly how I got started.

What was wonderful about this specific industry was that all schools that required training programs for their students had to put up a bid on a government business portal, GeBiz. That was the best thing about this business. Every single day, I would get an email, showcasing how many schools required a training program on leadership, study skills, team bonding, outdoor and indoor camps, etc. Leads would flow into my email inbox on a daily basis. The only challenge I had was to stand out from a sea of competition. Early on, I learnt the importance of developing a brand that my prospective clients could recognize. However, this blessing came at a cost. While my focus on branding strengthened early on, I failed to exercise the muscle that would be crucial for me to succeed as I pivoted from training students in schools to employees in corporate organizations.

After five years of working with students, I chose to write my first book, *Empowering Millennials*, to guide youths on the pathway to adulting effectively. The book was written for university graduates and new entrants to the workforce. However, the book attracted the attention of the media which then amplified my visibility and attracted the attention of managers who were struggling to manage the Millennial generation. Within a month of my book launch, I found myself speaking to corporate organizations and associations about the topic of Millennials. However, as the initial buzz of the book launch died down, as the number of speaking enquiries dwindled down, I found myself with a new realization. GeBiz was great for me to start out in business, but as I moved out of that space, I realized I was missing an asset like GeBiz. An asset that would drop a good number of leads and enquiries into my inbox for me to send proposals to. That was also the moment I realized that while I had experience with drafting proposals and closing sales, I knew absolutely nothing about marketing. Zero. Zilch. Nada. I had no clue where my next client was coming from, and it kept me awake at night.

That realization kickstarted my (now) obsession with marketing, branding, and sales. It inspired me to go deep into understanding the psychology of the people I wanted to attract like bees to honey. I knew I needed a system to be in place to generate highly qualified, high-quality leads. I appreciated the power of having high-quality leads. During my GeBiz days, it made rejections sting less as there was a long list of qualified leads to send proposals to. It was at this moment I realized the value of the quote I mentioned first.

Attention is the most valuable currency in business. In other words, no attention, no business. I knew I needed a marketing system and I knew I needed one that churned out a high number of highly qualified leads, just like GeBiz. Over the years of experimenting and getting burned, I slowly picked up the pieces that worked which I have now poured into this book for you to benefit from.

What's Complicated for You is Intuitive for Me

You've probably noticed this yourself. Preferences have changed drastically amongst the younger generations. What appeals to the Millennials and Gen Zs completely befuddle the Baby Boomers and Gen Xers. Whether it is music, movies, or brands, many of the older generations cannot relate to the brand icons and influencers that the younger generations look up to. The older generations still feel more comfortable to look up newspapers and head over to shopping malls to make a purchase, although they are shifting towards digital means of purchases as well. They still relish the company of a good salesperson who can educate them on the products and are willing to make the purchase if they are impressed by the product and the showmanship of the salesperson. For the older generation, the older times were simpler times. In other words, it means they didn't feel as stressed trying to buy groceries from a smartphone application. As a speaker, there are countless stories I've heard from leaders and participants who have come up to me to share their anxiety in keeping up with technology. It is bewildering for many from the older generation to see Millennials simply orchestrate their purchase of flight tickets through their phones by flicking, swiping, and even multi-tasking at the same time.

It's almost as if they didn't have to think through the steps (they probably didn't). Perhaps this is why Millennials are known as the digital natives.

There are about four generations of consumers in the world today.

Generations	Years
Baby Boomers	1946–1964
Gen X	1965–1979
Millennials	1980–1995
Gen Z	1996–2010

Now I know what you may be thinking. Isn't Gen Z different from the Millennials? No, not drastically, from a marketing point of view. Baby Boomers are more similar to Gen Xers just in the same way as Millennials are to Gen Zs. It is the gap between the older generations (Baby Boomers and Gen Xers) and the younger generations (Millennials and Gen Zs) that has widened during the decades where technology accelerated at incredible speeds. It influenced the behaviours of the younger generations as they grew up. It has completely changed the way we think, rationalize and make purchases.[4] It has revolutionized the way we relate to brands because our values have also changed along the way. The rate of technological adoption makes it wrong to see an entire generation that spans over fifteen years as being the same. There is bound to be nuanced differences even within the generation, and it is important that we become aware of this. There is undoubtedly a conflict of interests and priorities that needs to be overcome, but there are also many unexpected similarities and shared values. It is up to us as marketers to look past the assumptions about youth culture and listen to this cohort when they tell you how they experience the world. Learn from their perspective, embrace the conflicts and differences, or face the consequences.

---

[4] G.L. Witt, & Baird, D. E., *Gen Z Frequency: How Brands Tune in And Build Credibility*. (KOGAN PAGE, 2021)

Three Waves of Millennials

- Wave 1: Xennial/Geriatric Millennial: 1979–1985
  It's interesting to see that even though Millennials are thought to be pretty similar, there are some nuances that can be noticed amongst those who were born closer to the 1980s. They are known as the Xennials, or Geriatric Millennial, who uniquely bridge the divide between digital natives and digital adapters. Here's why:
  The speed of technological adoption makes it wrong to see the entire Millennial generation that spans over almost twenty years as being the same. Children from the early 1980s spent their formative years on both sides of the analog and digital divide, and play a crucial role in helping bridge the communication gaps between the adapters and the natives. They know what a pager and a fax machine is and are privy to the fact that phones came with wires in the early days. Music was portable through the Sony Walkman which carried a small number of songs.
  There is a sense of anxiety that comes with using technology based on the number of years you have used technology as your primary means of communication. We see this anxiety more prominently in our interactions with members of the Baby Boomer and Gen X generations. It takes a lot of concerted effort to spend time in the digital and social media space using the latest devices. We have to 'catch up' with the younger ones who seem to have less anxiety using digital devices. This group has seen both sides.

- Wave 2: Millennials: 1986–1995
  The second wave of Millennials are seen as the ones who got their hands on their first mobile phone when they were children or in their teenage years. They witnessed the first computer, mobile phone with keypads and the smartphone. Connecting to the internet began with a tech-sounding dial up tone. If you got any phone calls while you were surfing the internet,

your internet would get disconnected. It also worked the other way around. If your mother was hogging the phone for the last three hours, it meant there was no way you could connect to the internet. Growing up, Millennials enjoyed music through the discman which held more songs than the walkman. They enjoyed gaming, MSN, and MTV in their younger days for entertainment. As technology progressed, they formed their own digital avatar when social media companies like Facebook, Instagram, and Twitter sprouted in the 2000s. This group became comfortable with treating Google as their go-to buddy for all the questions they needed answers to. This group came of age when Google became a verb.

- Wave 3: Gen Z: 1996–2010 (Millennials on steroids)
  You know the funny thing about the average person on the street? They think all young people are Millennials (lol). It's a common misconception that people have because some people have come to misunderstand Millennials as a synonym for young adults. How do I know this? I've gotten many parents coming to me for advice on how to manage their Millennial teenagers. The thing they fail to understand is that being a Millennial is not a phase. When you're identified with a generation, you don't grow out of it like a caterpillar that goes through the different phases before becoming a butterfly. The understanding on the ground is that all young people are known as Millennials and I don't blame them. When we see pictures, memes, and videos of Millennials, we see young people. At the same time, it's very difficult to distinguish the oldest Gen Z (twenty-seven, as of 2023) with the youngest Millennial (twenty-eight, as of 2023).

  While technically Gen Zs don't fall under the Millennial generation category, it can be argued that they have more in common with Millennials than they do with Gen X or Baby Boomers. The generation gap, which always existed even before Millennials were born, really widened during the time when

Millennials were growing up. That's why Millennials take all the brunt for their 'newer' behaviours or expectations. See the illustration below for a better understanding of the widened generational gap.

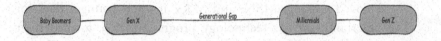

The term 'Millennial' has become the moniker that is commonly used to refer to all youths in their early twenties to early thirties. As a marketer, this is an important understanding of the layman. The layman doesn't really dive deep into generational specifics, and they categorize youths differently. Even before I entered this space of studying generations, I thought I was a Gen Y, and 'Millennials' was the term used for those born after the millennium i.e. year 2000. How wrong I was!

I categorize Gen Zs as the Wave 3 Millennials because of the nuanced differences amongst them. The Gen Zs grew up in a world where technology was rapidly developing and they got their hands on the latest smartphone in their early childhood. They understand how to navigate these devices intuitively and look to TikTok and YouTube for answers to their questions. Instead of Google, this group leans in to TikTok for answers because they love how its algorithm works in their favour. They are very aware of the brands that stand for the same values as them and support them wholeheartedly. They don't remember 9/11 as an in-person experience. They only learned about it in history class or from a parent who shared that experience. They don't have the same fear and uncertainty that unfolded from this event. For Gen Zs, Covid-19 has become the defining moment thus far. In other words, are Gen Zs different from Millennials? Yes. But are the differences huge? I don't think so, and hence, they fit in really well as Wave 3.

Why Focus on Millennials? What about the Other Generations?

Demographic Influence

As Baby Boomers retire, they cease to be the most influential generation. This means the social, political and economic terrain will be reshaped for the next several decades. Millennials are now the largest adult cohort worldwide, spanning 1.8 billion people. That is roughly about 23 per cent of the global population. According to WeForum, Asia is unmatched when it comes to Millennials with 1.1 billion in the region. Consider that for a moment—this generation is about to dominate the consumer market. Baby Boomers used to dominate marketing preferences. Not anymore, despite having more money on hand in their prime years. It's because Millennials have long term potential from a marketing point of view. Gen X was too small of a generation to be targeted when Millennials turned out to be a bigger generation than Gen X. If that is not enough to convince your company to shift your marketing research focus from the Baby Boomer generation to the influential Millennial generation, well, read on. There hasn't been a fixation on marketing to a specific generation since the Baby Boomers, and so many consumers outside of this demographic are left wondering why they are being ignored. In fact, older generations are currently in their prime when it comes to spending ability. However, many are asking themselves, *'Why isn't my money seen as valuable as Millennials?'*

Well, it's all about long term potential. Millennials haven't even reached their full buying power yet compared to the Gen Xers and Baby Boomers and yet, their buying power eclipses that of other generations. In other words, they are the most lucrative market. Nearly every marketer today is making it a point to make Millennials a priority and have started leaning in to understand what drives and delights this instrumental group. Millennials and Gen Zs are projected to make up 75 per cent of the Association of Southeast Asian Nations (ASEAN) consumers by 2030. Demographic forces have a powerful influence on society. For instance, investors are placing a greater focus on sustainable practices, with alternative energy innovations and solutions taking priority. It's becoming clear that as social dialogues change, investing choices follow and this presents a critical opportunity for businesses who are adapting to match the requirements of the younger generation.[5]

Economic Influence

Companies that win Millennial businesses stand to enjoy robust economic growth for years to come. In 2015, Millennials surpassed Baby Boomers as the largest living generation in the United States alone. Millennials already spend $1 trillion, and that spending power will increase as their income reaches $8.3 trillion by 2025. Comparatively, Gen Xers only have a spending power of $6.4 trillion, Baby Boomers have a spending power of $1.1 trillion and Gen Zs (those that have entered the workforce) have a spending power of $360 billion. According to Daymon Worldwide, only 29 per cent of Millennials will buy the same brand. This is a lower brand loyalty score when you compare it with the previous generations. What this means is brands must do more to attract and keep Millennial customers which means companies have to constantly be innovating in their marketing and service departments. This group has minimal tolerance for companies that haven't taken the time and effort to get to know them. Whether you are a global company or a startup, the same rules apply.

The Great Wealth Transfer

As the Baby Boomers retire, guess who they're giving their generational wealth to? Yes, the Millennials. It's being named as 'The Great Wealth Transfer' where the Baby Boomers leave their generational wealth to the Millennials. This demographic will inherit trillions of dollars and will have potential spending power unlike we've ever imagined. Between Bill Gates' pledge to give 'virtually all' of his wealth away and Patagonia

---

[5] Dorothy Neufeld, 'There are 1.8 billion Millennials on earth. Here's where they live', *World Economic Forum*, 8 November 2021 (https://www.weforum. org/agenda/2021/11/millennials-world-regional-breakdown/)

founder Yvon Chouinard's decision to donate his entire company to fight climate change, it is becoming clear that views of inherited wealth have changed. These high profile pledges are happening as part of the greatest generational wealth transfer, with Baby Boomers set to pass their children more than $68 trillion.

Baby Boomers enjoyed the returns of the economy that they invested in. In a post-Second World War world, the Baby Boomers' working and living experiences were that of great prosperity. Their parents had already made sacrifices during the war years to give them a better life and had paid all the taxes necessary to keep university tuition low, which meant as young adults entering the workforce for the first time, Boomers could graduate with little to no debt. At the same time, housing was plentiful post-war, and strong labour protections meant even high school graduates could afford to buy their first homes on a minimum hourly rate salary. These homes then continued to appreciate in value over time, and decades of economic growth followed for the boomers. So much so that by 2020, records show that the Baby Boomer generation held approximately 57 per cent of all wealth and assets in the US economy. In comparison, millennials held just 3 per cent of the country's entire wealth. So imagine this generation going from holding a mere 3 per cent to approximately 60 per cent of the entire wealth in the US economy in the near future.

Over time, Baby Boomers' wealth simply grew while costs remained low. As a result, they have a good lump sum of savings that they are passing over to their children as inheritance after their time is up. Most companies will need a strategy to attract younger consumers, employees, and investors. A brand refresh won't suffice. Companies will need to rethink their entire operating model and value proposition. As Brian A. Kuz, CMO of Talking Rain Beverage Co says, 'The question becomes, will Millennials be brand focused and spend, or will they be cause-focused, save the world, cure cancer, stop world hunger, or will they save, just as their Baby Boomer parents did?' The great wealth transfer represents a once-in-a-lifetime opportunity for brands to capture the hearts and minds of young consumers, employees, and investors. On the flip side, it poses a substantial threat to brands that fail to adapt to the speed of change.

Social Influence

According to Pew Research, almost all Millennials (nearly 100 per cent) now say they use the internet. Having grown up with or only slightly before the internet, Millennials are not shy about using technology. This is good news especially for brands that use technology to sell or brands that sell technology. Nine out of Ten Millennials have a smartphone. With the widespread device ownership use comes a higher likelihood of consuming web content. Millennials have become a lot more complex as a consumer. Long before the term 'influencer' was coined, young people played that role by creating and interpreting trends. Now a generation of influencers have come on to the scene.

They are the digital natives who, from their earliest youth, have been exposed to the internet, to social networks, and to mobile systems. This development in technology has produced a hypercognitive generation that is very comfortable with collecting and cross-referencing many sources of information while integrating virtual and offline experiences. It has also empowered them to mobilize themselves for a variety of causes in search of truth. They make decisions in a highly analytical and pragmatic way. They are well networked and have a knack of organizing themselves through social media for a common cause. Millennials are known to reject companies without a clear and relatable brand story and content. They are concerned about having their privacy protected, being listened to or respected by brands, and the reliability of brands they choose. You have to remember, Millennials grew up surrounded by advertising anywhere and everywhere they go, so they're not going to be fooled by marketing messages. The onslaught of media has massively desensitized Millennials to any traditional advertising strategies. They know the importance of their demographic to company sales and they aren't going to play into advertising tactics, schemes, or games unless they have some real substance.

They seek brands that connect with their passions and interests and contribute to their lives, or support them in whatever they're trying to do. They like brands that inspire them to push forward, to reach further to achieve their dreams, and to find and inspire new and unique solutions for them. They enjoy brands that provide experiences that create a community, a place of belonging, or something for them to be a part of, or that they can share and be excited about. In 2018, when Kylie Jenner tweeted, 'Does anyone still use Snapchat anymore', she set off a downward spiral for Snapchat's stock. A headline from CNN Money read: 'Snapchat loses $1.3 billion after Kylie Jenner tweet'.

The Impressionability Factor

Ever since the Covid-19 pandemic, consumers have altered their everyday behaviour in many striking ways. Simple things such as where they work to how they occupy their leisure hours to what they buy have changed. Leading the way in making these changes are the generations of consumers who are most adventurous and least settled in their ways—the Millennials and Gen Zs. Their impressionability is a golden opportunity for marketers. How can marketers take advantage of this moment of disruption when consumer behaviours and loyalties are in flux and when new longer-term behaviours, loyalties, and spending preferences may emerge? The economic, social and technological disruptions trigger dramatic and permanent changes in consumer behaviours, creating unique challenges and opportunities for brands.

Trends in Marketing

The US presidential elections are one of the biggest trend-setting moments in marketing history because of one thing: It is one of the most fiercely contested marketing campaigns there is around the world. It's like the Formula 1 of marketing. In 1933, US President elect Franklin Roosevelt did something very unique known as the fireside chat on national radio. This launched the radio device as the dominant channel for marketing—shifting away from newspaper print. Then in the 1960s President elect John F. Kennedy had a debate with Nixon which was on live television which then kickstarted the trend of television as the main source of marketing to communicate with the people. The TV dominated the presidential elections for a few years until technology caught up and then President elect Obama came up with a social media campaign called 'Obama Everywhere'. The Obama '08 campaign was all about marketing to people through social media. He was omnipresent on Twitter, Facebook, and YouTube (the other 'missing' platforms weren't up back then). After that, we saw this company called Cambridge Analytica that used questionable methods to help Trump win the elections. Cambridge Analytica is known to have collected huge amounts of data from Facebook and they would personalize their ads. They would crunch the data and deliver the message that they knew you wanted to hear via ads which is completely different to what your neighbour would have seen on Facebook. So someone who really cared about health and welfare would get ads from Trump that talked about the subject. Those who cared about guns and the rights around that would get ads on that topic featuring Trump. In short, the data collected allowed the president elect to personalize the message they were sending to different parts of the country in order to win votes.

The Age of Hyper-Personalization

When we see new forms of marketing campaigns happening in the US presidential elections, we can actually predict this to be the dominant trend until something major comes along to disrupt it. Personalization, which was the marketing word of the year 2019, is now becoming a big trend and at the moment, only large companies know how to capture the right data and crunch insights from it. The big companies are winning through data analytics and the smaller companies will have to start to learn how to leverage on collecting data and giving a personalized experience based on the data collected.

As we know now, we have things like artificial intelligence on the rise. I imagine the future of the US presidential elections to be hyper-personalized. Every single person will be able to receive a personalized video addressing them by name while discussing the issues that matter to them. All of this would probably be completely A.I.-generated—influencing all by a deep fake video using the script that is based on the data they know about you as an individual. Your neighbour, of course, will get a completely different *deepfake* video talking about topics entirely different to what you received. I won't be too surprised if the video shows you a bit of the Metaverse at the same time.

Currently, if you're a small business, it's easy to personalize when you don't have a large number of people to reach out to. A lot of small businesses have this advantage of personalizing, because they know the names of their customers and their preferences. Small businesses knew stuff about you because of the conversations that were exchanged frequently between one another. Big companies didn't have this advantage. They played on a one-size-fits-all message for a long time until personalization became possible at scale. Big companies today have figured out how to automate personalization and are currently in a better position to beat small businesses with a personalized feel. Take Amazon for instance. It is a big business that has created a personalized shopping experience for the end user based on their past shopping habits. Sometimes they still get it wrong but most times they get it right. Shopify is another company that has personalization built into it. Facebook and all the other social media platforms that empowers users to sell to one another rely on personalization to suggest your products to customers who have similar product- or service-purchase history.

If you want to win over this generation of consumers, you have to leverage the tools that allow you to hyper-personalize and get recommended to this group. This is a generation that prefers their phone to the laptop. This is where social media comes in. It is no longer about broadcasting to the masses with a single message. It's about leveraging the tools and algorithms that allow you attract your tribe. This means you have to first start with mediums that allow you to do that. In other words, digital is going to be the space to dominate because of the advantage of hyper-personalization. It might seem like a very technical and challenging thing to do, but trust me, this is where we are headed. You can either paddle hard and catch the wave or float around and see what happens. It's totally up to you.

> 'A lot of times you don't even have to search for what you're looking for on social media. It's just there.'
>
> —Jamie Tan, *Millennial*

According to the author of *Instabrain*, Sarah Weise, 85 per cent of the young generation find out about new products through social media. Their discovery is mostly through people i.e. influencers, friends, family who are promoting something that has been really useful for them without being paid to market it. The content on social media provides information about where to buy the clothing and accessories, where to buy books, and how to manage your time. With social media, we not only have influencers with millions of followers, we also have micro-influencers who only have social media audiences ranging from tens of thousands to hundreds of thousands of followers and nano influencers with as few as a thousand followers. In fact, the nano-influencers are the ones who are most approached by brands and young consumers alike. Their lack of fame is seen as one of the qualities that make them approachable. They are easier to deal with and are seen as being more authentic by their followers.

Leveraging Post-pandemic Behaviours

The rise of high speed internet in the early 2000s and of smartphones a decade later led to a boom in e-commerce and video streaming that has permanently altered the retail and media landscape. After the SARS outbreak in 2002–2003, China saw a fivefold increase in its rate of e-commerce penetration. After the global financial crisis of 2008–2009, we saw a disruption in the retail landscape, giving rise to price-conscious habits amongst consumers who opted for e-commerce retailers over traditional supermarkets. From 2009 to 2019, e-commerce penetration in retail rose by more than 10 per cent in the US and UK, and 7 per cent in France. With the Covid-19 pandemic, brands must reassess their marketing strategies and expenditures. While prior crises offer a multitude of useful lessons, in many ways the current environment is unique.

Unlike recent economic downturns, the Covid-19 pandemic is not merely a financial crisis. It is also a health crisis with unprecedented impacts on society, such as social distancing and business closures. It comes at a time when massive shifts are happening in purchasing and media consumption behaviours thanks to technology. As such, we can expect the pandemic to have a more significant impact on consumer behaviours than previous crises did. In addition to changing what products the younger consumers buy, they are also changing where they buy from. Most Millennial consumers are expected to increase their overall spending through online means. Those who started ordering groceries online for the first time during the pandemic lockdowns enjoyed the convenience of it and emphasized they will continue to make purchases of groceries in the same way moving forward. Among other retailers, online marketplaces are expected to be winners with Millennial consumers in the new normal.

During a crisis, when younger generations experience the most dramatic shifts in behaviour and spending, these consumers become even more critical than in normal times. Smart companies will develop a deep understanding of Millennial consumers, anticipate their shifts, and adjust their marketing strategies in order to catch the wave early. Those that act quickly and aggressively with the right moves stand to gain immediate and lasting benefits. That's why it is critical for brands to look at defining a winning strategy for Millennial consumers.

A Different Approach

Being a 5G marketer is not about forgetting everything you've learnt until now about marketing. It is about looking at everything against the backdrop of dizzyingly fast-paced transformation happening in the marketing landscape and the current crisis we are in. It is about reinventing, reimagining, and reinvigorating marketing, to make it an even stronger force that drives the business momentum. If you want to win the loyalty of this generation, you have to understand that they demand a completely different approach. You need to understand the new set of rules for marketing and brand-building to connect with this critical consumer group. That means that you must be willing to unlearn, learn and relearn as a marketer. You have to be willing to let go of what you knew to be true and be willing to experiment with what lies ahead. You have to be willing to innovate instead of improve. Data is the new oil. You have to learn to leverage this to build influence and clout amongst your group of targeted customers. They don't want ads anymore. In fact, they are blocking them from their screens with the help of ad blockers and even paying to be in ad-free environments. We are currently in unchartered territory, a world that is full of creativity, innovation, and incredible opportunity.

Companies need to listen to Millennials, from a business point of view. It is the act of consciously paying attention to them, with an attempt to understand, to consider, and of thinking about what is important to them instead of what may be important to you. Basically, companies need to care about what Millennials have to say. They want to be talked to, not talked at. That means you listen, understand, and then communicate as opposed to simply assuming you know what they want. Companies that don't bother to understand how this largest generation of consumers think, research, purchase and communicate will end up as relics and stories shared by university professors in marketing courses or keynote speakers in business conferences. Your journey to learn more about this group today could mean the difference between future success or failure. The way a company can leverage marketing to its full potential and turn it into a business driver and a brand builder will prove to be a crucial advantage. The last five years has seen more change in marketing than the last fifty. Not surprisingly, the next five years outpace all of them put together. It is both exciting and daunting.

With this book, I hope to inspire you to focus on the Millennials in a strategic manner. The time to dive deep into research is now. This large and financially-responsible group holds a never-seen-before influence over our consumer markets. Yet, marketing to this group of highly educated consumers will not be child's play. They have high standards for themselves and higher standards for the brands who want to win their vote. As I keep repeating, brand loyalty with this group is a lot harder to achieve than any of the previous generations. This book will challenge your thinking and guide you towards mastering the new marketing mindset to engage with the Millennials. It offers you the blueprint to build an engaged following by deeply understanding the psychology of the Millennials and leveraging on that data to achieve the business results you are aiming for. So if that's what you're looking for, let's begin.

Welcome to *Marketing to Millennials*!

Chapter 2

Are You Leaving Money on the Table by Making These Marketing Mistakes?

In any industry, there are businesses that people line up for their product or service. There are restaurants people don't mind queueing up for, products people line up for overnight to get their hands on it and tickets that simply sell out hours after its release. There are speakers and consultants who are booked six months in advance while charging ten times more than others. Even for stuff like furniture, there are companies that only allow you to pre-order. Simply put, when you get your marketing right, you become part of the companies where you don't chase clients. Clients chase them instead.

It's a beautiful position to be in. To be wanted, to be desired. To be selective of the clients you pick and choose to work with. It is about generating demand to a point it outstrips supply. It is when people want something more than the allotted capacity. With the digital tools we have at our disposal, it has become easier to orchestrate the same results. All you need is a deeper understanding of the Millennial mindset and how they transform from loyal fans and followers to die-hard customers. We live in remarkable, changing times. Many ideas that worked five years ago aren't working anymore. Every marketer is under pressure to get creative, innovate and put results on the board.

The pace of change is speeding up and the way the world of business and society works won't look the same in ten years from now.

In order for you to stay relevant as a marketer, it is important to ditch the old marketing principles that no longer serve you and embrace the new. Just look at the corporate graveyard—giants like Toys R Us, Blockbuster, Borders Books & Music, Kodak, Palm Pilot, Google Plus, and many more. They were tied to the tactics of the past. These brands and products failed to pay attention to the coming tide of customer needs and expectations. Have you ever wondered, what if product owners and executive decision makers had taken another direction instead? Would things have turned out differently? Truth is, we will never know. What we do know is that these particular brands did not pay attention to the trends and needs of future customers, and how those future customers were impacting the expectations of existing customers. The first step to embracing the new mindset of marketing starts with letting go of the mistakes that hold us back as marketers. Gone are the days where emphasizing on a product's quality, price point or 'wow' factor makes a difference in sales. Throw those old ideas and tactics out of the window. Your new objective is to connect with young people on a human level. The key is knowing what approach to take, or at least, what approach not to take. And that's what this chapter is all about.

Mistake #1: Treating Them Like Any Other Generation i.e. Not Having a Millennial-centric Marketing Strategy

The key topic on every marketer's mind right now is how to effectively and efficiently market to Millennials, but the issue is that very few of those marketers truly understand [this diverse] group. More research dollars are going against this group than against Hispanic marketing or even marketing to current demographics of a brand. Why? Purchase power. This demographic will inherit trillions of dollars and will have a potential spending power unlike we've ever imagined. The question becomes, will they be brand focused and spend or will they be cause focused (save the world, cure cancer, stop world hunger), or will they save, just like their Baby Boomer parents did? It's a guessing game. The brand who first finds the key to unlock the door to discover the mystery behind this group wins. Others will surely perish.'[6]

You can probably assume that marketing to this generation of consumers has a lot of similarities to marketing to every other generation. On some level, you would be correct. They have a need to be met, and many of the marketing truths you've come to know will work on this group. Let's be frank, though: Millennials are a diverse generation, so it's impossible to make any sort of monolithic statement about them. What appeals to one millennial may not resonate with another. Still, as a group, they have enough characteristics in common that it's possible to make some general statements. That's why looking at what behaviours they do share is an essential part of constructing a brand specifically with them in mind. You would be wise to understand the unique traits of Millennials regarding how they buy things. Moreover, their values and life goals are dramatically different from those of previous generations. Rather than focusing on material possessions and status, they tend to prioritize happiness and life experiences. By considering their impact and making them feel heard, companies can form relationships to highlight their expertise and earn trust from this demographic along the way. When looking at consumer spending by generation, Millennials exhibit distinguished shopping behaviours.

One major mistake marketing professionals make is treating Millennials like other generations that have come before them, especially in their marketing efforts. Instead, you need to first recognize that they are different from earlier generations in several ways. Millennials are the next 'Baby Boomers'; a group of people so valuable that advertisers are dropping their existing methods to cater to them. This generation is halfway between the last years of the classroom and the workplace. They are the most knowledgeable of all generations, with nearly 25 per cent having post-secondary education. Companies

6 Kuz, B. A., '27 Expert Tips for Marketing to Millennials', *INC.*, (Retrieved 4 May 2023, from https://www.inc.com/christina-desmarais/27-expert-tips-for-marketing-to-millennials.html)

are finding that traditional advertisements are becoming less effective as a means to entice Millennial shoppers. This group researches online, tests products in the stores, seeks out honest reviews by their peers and makes their purchases online. They are less likely to buy something online if the website looks dated, even if they really like the item. This is a generation that is constantly buying, selling and sharing products and services they believe in. And where they are buying, they are also influencing others at the same time through Yelp and Google reviews. Even if Millennials spend a mere $10 on a meal somewhere, they are letting hundreds of people on the internet know what they think. This behaviour is so specific to this group that brands have to learn to leverage this behaviour for better marketing reach at no cost.

They think differently about how someone should make money and how corporations should treat employees and customers. This group is usually associated with a more progressive view. The 'Millennial way of thinking' varies quite significantly from their parents, grandparents, and traditional corporate views. They are considered to have views that are more decentralized i.e. they don't automatically follow societal norms and instead conduct research to develop their own opinions. Corporate structures usually have a more centralized view, one that is less personalized and focuses on a mass-market approach. As marketing begins to adopt more of a personalized approach with the help of social media, Millennials are beginning to expect that personalization as they interact with brands and look to purchase a particular product or service. Companies with an efficient social media presence and those that customize the shopping experience find that young adults will return. This is why more marketers are leaning towards social media platforms and digital technology to get their marketing messages to cut through the clutter in a non-interruptive way.

Millennials are the first generation to have experienced much of their lives with the internet, and many of them express a desire to work specifically with authentic, honest brands. While older generations may have accepted a more corporate feel, Millennials will keep searching until they find the personable brand they can trust. By gaining an understanding of this group and sharing content that they'd enjoy, you can market to them more effectively. Seventy-three per cent of millennials report that they would rather have digital experiences with their banks than personal ones. Compared to older generations, Millennials are most likely to use online-and mobile-banking channels due to easy use websites and great apps.

Millennials are spending an average of 242 minutes online or using apps per day, and they're craving content-driven media. They're scouring websites, blogs, and social media because they feel empowered by all of the remarkable content they're discovering. They're also sharing, liking, pinning, tweeting, snapping, forwarding, and commenting on all of their findings to impart this sense of empowerment to the online community. So, what makes this type of content really resonate with this group? Millennials trust what they feel is authentic.

Interacting in a user-centric environment is what engages them, as 90 per cent of Millennials say authenticity is important to them when deciding which brands they support. Today, young shoppers' attitudes and behaviour are largely inspired by people they know in person or online, or even strangers who share their interests on social networks. Millennials carry these 'advisors' with them on their smartphones and everywhere they go. They trust relevant, authentic opinions from real product users they can relate to. In fact, Millennials believe that user-generated content is 35 per cent more memorable than other media.

Technology equals convenience for Millennials. Investing in Millennial engagement involves finding the right balance between traditional and digital experiences. As the world becomes increasingly more digital, opportunities to exceed Millennial expectations grow. The smart brands are ditching traditional ads, focusing on design, and leveraging social media and technology like rock stars. There's no arguing that the Millennial generation possesses a lot of potential purchasing power and brand loyalty so a one-size-fits-all marketing approach won't work well if you're looking to attract the Millennials. The companies that do it right stand a much better chance to win market shares moving forward. Failing to tune in to this generation will only lead companies to leave money on the table.

Taking Shots in the Dark (Not Doing Your Research)

Many organizations assume they already know what their customers want, and as a result of that, they skip customer research. This can lead to poor decisions that fail to meet customers' needs. Assuming they know what customers want without conducting research: A large retail chain may assume that their customers are primarily interested in low prices and so may not conduct research to understand other aspects of customer behaviour such as their preferences for customer service or product quality. Blockbuster Video assumed that their customers wanted to rent movies in-store, but failed to conduct research to understand changing customer preferences for online streaming. This led to the company's decline and eventual bankruptcy.

Other times, organizations conduct research that is too narrow in scope. When you only focus on specific aspects of customer behaviour or preferences without taking a comprehensive view, it leads to missed opportunities or misinterpretation of the data collected. A technology company may conduct research on their customer's satisfaction with their latest product, but fail to consider the broader context of how their customers use their products and the problems they face in their work or daily lives. PepsiCo conducted a market research study on their customers' preferences for a new beverage, but failed to consider the broader context of health and wellness trends, leading to the failure of their product line.

An automobile company may rely on research conducted several years ago that shows that their customers value safety above all else, and so they may not invest in other features that are important to customers today, such as fuel efficiency or entertainment technology. Today, Tesla manufactures computers on wheels and is taking over the automobile market, leaving established brands scrambling to catch up with their own line of electric cars.

Kodak relied on outdated research that showed customers preferred physical prints over digital photos, and so failed to invest in digital photography technology, leading to the company's decline. I notice organizations relying on outdated research that isn't relevant to the world and market conditions we live in today. When you rely on research that is outdated, assuming that the consumer preferences and behaviours haven't changed, it leads to missed opportunities and poorly executed campaigns.

Some organizations fail to listen to customer feedback, dismissing complaints or suggestions as irrelevant. This can lead to negative customer experiences and missed opportunities for improvement. A social media platform may dismiss user complaints about privacy violations, assuming that these complaints are irrelevant to the platform's success, leading to poor user experiences and negative brand perception. Facebook and Instagram have constantly borne the brunt of complaints over the high number of scammers creating fake accounts. This totally destroys the user experience. Imagine every month, you encounter reports from your network that someone is asking them for money under your name simply because they created a profile that looks exactly like yours, with your exact profile picture and images. United Airlines ignored customer complaints about poor treatment and service, leading to a public relations crisis and significant loss of customer trust and loyalty.

Some organizations conduct research without clear goals or objectives in mind. This can lead to irrelevant data or difficulty in analyzing the results. An e-commerce company may conduct a survey asking customers about their shopping habits, but without clear goals for what they hope to achieve with this information, they may struggle to interpret the data or to apply it to their business strategy. Uber failed to involve drivers in the research process when they made changes to their driver compensation model, leading to backlash and protests from drivers. There are organizations that conduct research without involving customers in the process. A healthcare provider may conduct research to understand patients' experiences, but without involving patients in the research process, they may not fully understand the patient perspective or their needs.

Ford conducted research on customer preferences for electric vehicles, but failed to share the findings with all teams, resulting in delays in their electric vehicle development. Some organizations conduct research but fail to share the findings across the organization. This can lead to missed opportunities for collaboration or improvement.

A financial services company may conduct research on their customers' attitudes toward digital banking, but without sharing the findings across the organization, other teams may not understand the insights gained from the research and may not be able to act on them.

Microsoft relied solely on sales data to inform their product development strategy for their Zune media player, but failed to consider qualitative research such as focus groups or interviews, leading to the failure of the product. There are organizations that focus solely on quantitative research, such as surveys or analytics, without considering qualitative research. This can lead to a lack of understanding of the context behind the data. A consumer goods company may rely solely on sales data to inform their product development strategy, but without considering qualitative research such as focus groups or interviews, they may miss out on valuable insights into customer needs and preferences.

Amazon failed to follow up with customers who reported counterfeit products, leading to negative customer experiences and loss of trust in the company. Some organizations fail to follow up with customers after conducting research, missing an opportunity to build relationships and gain deeper insights into their needs and preferences. An online education platform may conduct a survey to understand student satisfaction with their courses, but without following up with individual students to gather more detailed feedback, they may miss an opportunity to address specific concerns and build stronger relationships with their customers.

Uber assumed that all customers were primarily motivated by low prices and convenience, and so failed to consider the importance of customer safety, leading to a public relations crisis and loss of customer trust. There are organizations that make assumptions about customer behaviour based on their own biases or experiences. This can lead to misinterpretation of the data and poor decision making.

Netflix made a series of unpopular decisions in 2011. First, they began with a price hike for all their services and then announced Netflix services will be divided into two: one for streaming and the other for DVD rentals. Each would get their own account information, login, passwords, and billing information. Plus the DVD mailing service was to be featured on a new site called 'Qwikster'.

Naturally, people were enraged. Guess what they did? They went to Facebook, Twitter, and forums to share their anger and frustrations. However, Netflix quickly recovered from their mishap of not listening. Netflix CEO Reed Hastings announced on a blog post stating,

> 'It is clear that for many of our members two websites would make things more difficult, so we are going to keep Netflix as one place to go for streaming and DVDs. This means no change: one website, one account, one password . . . in other words, no Qwikster. While the July price change was necessary, we are now done with price changes.'[7]

Instead of hiding away in his home, Hastings listened carefully and corrected the course immediately. He could have refused to change the policy and waited for people to get over the issue but he didn't. Instead, Hastings cut his losses quickly and salvaged the situation. As a result, after losing 800,000 customers after announcing Qwikster, he regained a net 610,000 customers in the fourth quarter of 2011. That's the power of listening.

Mistake #2: Not having a mobile-first marketing approach

Let's be honest: Millennials aren't influenced by traditional advertising tactics. Even if 'change is hard', most brands won't make headway if they continue along that mindset. As the years go by, we notice people are using their smartphones more and more, especially the younger ones. The youngest Millennials were still pre-teens when the first smartphones came out in the late 2000s. As such, they're the first generation of adults who are used to today's mobile-first method of navigating the world. While twenty years ago the primary purpose of the telephone was to make calls or send text messages, today it is also a window to the world. According to GSMA, the worldwide consortium of mobile operators, 2017 was a milestone year for the mobile industry,

---

[7] Bill Chappell, 'Netflix Kills Qwikster; Price Hike Lives On', *NPR*, (10 October 2011, https://www.npr.org/sections/thetwo-way/2011/10/10/141209082/netflix-kills-qwikster-price-hike-lives-on)

with the number of people connected to mobile services surpassing five billion, and those consuming internet services exceeding three billion. Although many millennials own a desktop, the average Millennial spends about 211 minutes on a smartphone per day, compared to only thirty-one minutes of desktop use.[8]

From scanning news headlines on your iPad before going to sleep to using a mobile app to find an indian restaurant with the highest number of 5-star reviews, to browsing this month's best streaming videos, all of the above-mentioned activities have become a habitual part of our lives. Google names these instances where we automatically grab our phone to look up something or take any kind of action as 'micro-moments'. As society truly becomes 'mobile-first', these micro-moments are now intertwined with our daily lives. We are now reflexively turning to our devices for answers and solutions. This is to be expected, being in the 'on-demand' economy where customers expect to have answers at their fingertips 24/7. With our increasing dependence on smartphones, the consumer journey has been fractured into hundreds of real-time, intent-driven micro-moments. Each micro-moment is a critical opportunity for brands to shape our decisions and preferences. With more people interacting, socializing, and shopping online, the number of potential 'touches' has undoubtedly grown exponentially since 2020. An average smartphone user checks his phone sixty-three times a day. That's a huge opportunity marketers are missing if they aren't making themselves visible on the mobile phone.[9]

To market towards Millennials, you need to understand smartphones from their perspective. Millennials grew up with smartphones and they act as the hub for their human relationships.

---

[8] Katt Boogard, 'Marketing to Millennials: 8 Strategic Tips to Success', *Wrike*, (5 July 2022 https://www.wrike.com/blog/millennial-top-marketing-strategies/#Advertising-to-millennials-top-tips).

[9] Jessica Hawthorne-Castro, 'Consumers Are Checking Their Phones 60 Times a Day. Here's How to Monetize These Micro-Moments', *Adweek*, (29 March 2021, https://www.adweek.com/performance-marketing/consumers-are-checking-their-phones-60-times-a-day-heres-how-to-monetize-these-micro-moments/)

They interact with their smartphones more than anything, or anyone else. Long story short, they trust their smartphones. In other words, Millennials live on mobile, so your brand should too.

Understanding your audience is key, but more importantly, integrating digital marketing strategies to appeal to this generation is quite another. As brands think about creating digital experiences, they must think about how every aspect of the experience works together— including a mobile first experience combined with great design and user experience. Keep on top of popular and emerging social media platforms to figure out how to best deliver your message to your consumers. Consider how to make your message as micro as best fits the mobile medium. A recent study by Annalect shows that 55 per cent of Millennials who own smartphones expect brands to have an app or mobile-friendly website. If your website content doesn't translate to mobile, you've lost them. Optimizing your landing pages for mobile so they load quickly is critical. Even on a small phone screen, there should be a clear call-to-action with minimum downtime.

The good news? Millennials are willing to listen to ads if you find them in the right spots. They are twice as likely to listen to a video ad on their smartphone than on television. Even better, people watching these videos are 1.8 times more likely to take action on the ad as people watching on their smartphones are more active and tend to research a product while they shop. Make sure your company's mobile experience is top-notch.

There is nothing that you cannot do with this device, be it paying bills, shopping online, playing games, listening to a favourite song, and anything else you can imagine. Thanks to Wi-Fi and free messaging applications, you can always make a call or chat with your favourite person. Information travels much faster than before thanks to both videos and images that can be sent today. Remember those days when there were only landlines, it took so much time to 'catch' a friend at home to tell him everything that happened that day. Today, it is possible to let a lot of people know what we are doing right away and even back it up with photos and videos. According to VOA News, 95 per cent of Millennials seem to dominate their category of smartphone usage and screen time. They reported having a smartphone or having access to one and 45 per cent reported they are online constantly. Millennials spend the most of their time on their phones with an average of 3.7 hours per day. 75 per cent use their mobile phones most often to search for products, compared to 16 per cent who use a computer. When it comes to online shopping, 68 per cent of Millennials use their phones most often, while 22 per cent use a computer.[10]

According to marketing expert Guru Gabriel Shaoolian, 'Mobile-first is a solution that meets user needs in the present while ensuring the website can accommodate the increasing multi-device future. Taking a mobile-first approach necessitates a lot of focus and attention on the needs of the user, and it requires the company to hone in on what is most essential about its message and its content. There's no room for flashy widgets and vanity features. In a way, the mobile-first approach offers the chance to strip away distractions and distill the experience down to what really matters.'[11]

Over 73 per cent of Millennials have become decision makers in purchasing products or services in their companies or their own businesses. Over 34 per cent are the sole decision makers regarding purchases. These B2B buyers have cited Internet search and vendor's websites as their top two means of researching products and services. 82 per cent of Millennial B2B buyers said mobile devices were important when researching new products and services. The mobile device has become a key instrument in helping them gather information up front by consuming information via social networks, videos, blogs, podcasts, etc.

Not having a mobile-first marketing approach in your marketing strategy will turn out to be a costly mistake. Your sales and marketing

---

[10] Maxwell Iskiev, ' How Each Generation Shops in 2023', *HubSpot*, (https://blog.hubspot.com/marketing/how-each-generation-shops-differently)

[11] G. Shaoolian, G, 'The shift from mobile-friendly to mobile-first: What your brand should know', *Forbes*, (https://www.forbes.com/sites/gabrielshaoolian/2017/07/13/the-shift-from-mobile-friendly-to-mobile-first-what-your-brand-should-know/?sh=40d100ae4626)

strategy must factor in the role of smartphones in everything from decision making and comparing options to making the final purchase decision. 93 per cent of people who use a mobile phone for research will then go on to make a purchase and one study even found that mobile accounts for 35 per cent of all retail ecommerce transactions. Mobile enables the confluence of different media streams with 84 per cent of smartphone and tablet users turning to their devices as they watch television, providing a huge opportunity for advertisement linking both television and mobile devices.

Mistake #3: Not Leveraging Social Media As a Part of Your Marketing Strategy

'Social-media presence is a badge of acceptance. Millennials are hungry for brand education via social media.'

—Hugh Rovit, CEO at Ellery Homestyles,
a supplier of ready-made window curtains
and top-of-bed products[12]

Whether they're following accounts that inspire them, perusing videos, researching products, or connecting with their favourite brands, the younger generation of consumers are clearly influenced by social media. More of them want to be influencers, start their own businesses, and get involved in new hobbies. Millennials will often go to social media platforms to learn and get advice before making a purchase or taking on a project. It's funny how we still see a lot of companies and business leaders are labelling social media platforms as pointless time wasters. Yet today, influencer marketing is poised to eat a real chunk of traditional marketing's lunch. More than three billion people around the world now use social media each month, with nine out of ten of those users accessing their chosen platforms via mobile devices. A recent study by Annalect shows that 47 per cent of Millennials claim that social media has helped introduce them to new brands.

---

[12] R. Hans, 'How to market to millennials in 2022', *Deskera Blog*. (Retrieved May 4, 2023, from https://www.deskera.com/blog/market-to-millennials/)

A whopping 71 per cent are more likely to buy from brands they 'like' on Facebook, or 'follow' on Twitter.[13]

Therefore, they are the first to notice if your digital experience is lacking. It's about using social media and technology in ways to create delightful experiences across all touchpoints—from design to content to customer support to creating seamless offline-to-online experience. Clearly, social media has a positive influence on business, regardless of whether it is specifically tied to ROI or bottom line. Of course, a robust social strategy is needed for experiential marketing and killer digital experiences. Social media monitoring tools are considered the norm in companies that want to stay ahead of the competition and anticipate consumers' needs. Proactive social listening can help brands access a vast amount of mentions on a specific topic, analyze them, and then use them to make predictions. Social listening can also determine the overall mood behind individual posts, providing brands with deeper insights into how people feel about something than ever before. Companies that provide such services monitor your social platforms together with your competitor's platforms. Brands can 'listen in' to conversations by people on products, services, or features they don't like. Focusing on the negative feedback gives brands the opportunity to move beyond the customer service to presenting solutions or alternatives. A whopping 70 per cent of Millennials are known to share feedback, ideas, opinions, and customer experiences on social media. This is a goldmine of data for marketers who are looking to monitor their perspective.[14]

Fifty per cent of Millennials have discovered new products on social media in the past three months, and 59 per cent of them say it's where they discover new products most often. They favour feed

[13] Lauren Friedman, 'Millennials And the Digital Experience', *Forbes*, (8 February 2017 https://www.forbes.com/sites/laurenfriedman/2017/02/08/millennials-and-the-digital-experience-getting-your-digital-act-together/?sh=40e666f5730d)

[14] Lauren Friedman, 'How Brands Can Spot the Next Millennial Pink', *Adobe Blog*, (9 December 2017 https://blog.adobe.com/en/publish/2017/09/12/brands-can-spot-next-millennial-pink)

posts, ads, and social media marketplaces when looking to discover new products. They also turn to influencers and social media shops to discover and buy things. According to Gary Vee, in his book, *Crushing It*, television viewership is declining across the board, while YouTube's daily viewership is rapidly approaching 1.25 billion hours per day. One in every five minutes spent on mobile is spent on social media. Every minute, 65,900 videos and photos are viewed on Instagram. Over three billion snaps are created each day on Snapchat, where over 60 per cent of ads are watched with audio on.

Influencer marketing has become a legitimate monetization strategy for anyone building a business. The top-grossing YouTubers earned a combined income of $70 million in 2016. Even with only a thousand followers, an entry-level Instagrammer could earn about $5,000 per year with just two posts a week. Just imagine what you could accomplish in your company with an entire team dedicated to social media? Almost all Millennials are connected, mostly through mobile devices. Social media has assumed an important role in many realms of young people's lives, beyond simply serving as a way of staying in touch with friends and family. It has become the top source of news compared to traditional sources such as TV, radio, or newspapers.

Social media has stopped becoming a medium of communication as Millennials have started treating social platforms as one-stop-shops for all of their daily needs. With the exponential increase of social media users and shifting consumption patterns, brands are leaving money on the table when they don't define a social media marketing strategy. Social media has become a dedicated marketing and sales channel. Active social media users have passed the 3.8 billion mark, increasing by more than 9 per cent year on year. The internet has opened a floodgate of opportunities to anyone willing to hustle to grow a fanbase through blogs and video channels to attract the attention of hundreds of thousands of brands. In a GlobalWebIndex survey, 48 per cent of respondents said that a discount followed by family and friend recommendations made them purchase a product, while only 17 per cent said they would buy because of an influencer or celebrity social media post. With social media anchored on connections and relationships, businesses will have greater opportunities to increase brand awareness and conversions when more Millennials advocate for their brand.

Mistake #4: Focusing on Brand Awareness Instead of Sales

'Brand awareness' is the term used to describe how familiar an individual is with a brand, product, or company. Companies spend considerable time and money building brand awareness but make a fatal mistake along the way. Back in the early days of advertising, awareness was the name of the game. Fifty years ago, if your brand could afford to get into television, print or radio advertising, you could dominate your category because you were one of the brands with high top-of-mind awareness. Awareness was all that mattered due to the lack of content and advertising clutter. There were just not that many big, advertised brands to remember. Today, if your business isn't a top fifty brand in the world, you should not be advertising with brand awareness as a goal. There is this misconception amongst traditional marketers that their role is purely to increase brand awareness. According to the author of *A New Marketer*, Maneesh Sah, the primary aim of marketing is to make it easier for sales teams to sell more. There is no point in having the best brand awareness initiatives if it isn't driving real conversations with real customers. The amount of impressions or brand awareness you create mean nothing today. Be real, care about customers created over sales generated and focus on building a sustainable community.

It is the conversations you have with the people that help consumers connect with your brand on a deeper level and get them thinking about purchasing your brand's products or services. Millennials are simply too informed for a brand impression alone to provide value to the business. In this new paradigm, the definition of frequency has also fundamentally changed. Frequency used to be about repeating the same exact message over and over and over again. Today, it is about finding a myriad of messages to get consumers to see you over and over again. Brand awareness focuses on mass appeal and getting in front of as many people as possible. It is not a metric that shows purchase intent, and is deemed fairly useless to the average brand.

Instead of focusing on mass marketing, Alex McEachern from Smile.io believes focusing on a niche and intimate demographic can help brands connect on an emotional level as opposed to a transactional level. A shift in focus from brand awareness to brand engagement is key to growing sales for the organization. If your brand allows for consumers to make purchases by creating accounts, it becomes a key indicator of brand engagement. The more customer interactions you generate through likes, comments and shares from social media, the more subscriptions to your blogs or email newsletters or YouTube channel, the more conversations your brand generates. All of these natural engagement points are much better indicators of how your brand is doing than the amount of times someone has potentially seen your content. The beauty of focusing on brand engagement is that it leads to a stronger community and a strong community leads to sustainable growth. With brand engagement, you start attracting consumers who are not just looking for the best price. Dale Carnegie said it best, 'You can close more business in two months by becoming interested in other people than you can in two years by trying to get people interested in you.'[15]

Mistake #5: Push Less And Pull More

In the past, outbound marketing methods like magazine ads, direct mail campaigns, and traditional media could get the word out there about your brand. However, Millennials are far less impressed by those marketing methods because they want to feel a connection with a brand before making a decision to purchase from them. Traditionally, companies focused on drawing in customers by mass posting ads on radio, TV and print. This traditional strategy is now being replaced by a more targeted, focused methodology. It is a strategy

---

[15] Dale Carnegie Quotes. (n.d.). *BrainyQuote.com*. Retrieved May 4, 2023, from BrainyQuote.com Website: https://www.brainyquote.com/quotes/dale_carnegie_156624

that focuses on building the brand's reputation, credibility, and trust to the point where potential customers are finding them. The advent of social networking and other interactive media is rapidly changing the advertising, marketing and sales landscapes. With smart devices we hold in our hands today, knowledge and information is easily accessible anywhere, anytime. This sounds overwhelming but it gives this generation of Millennials a unique advantage. Even marketers have taken notice.[16]

Companies have long trusted their traditional marketing strategies, otherwise known as 'push' marketing, where they promote a product or service through print advertisements and facilitating media coverage. A push campaign is when you take a product or service directly to consumers through ads or direct outreach. Traditional ads don't work anymore because 84 per cent of Millennials simply don't trust traditional advertising. They don't like the pushy, disingenuous nature of commercials and will do anything to within their power to skip, fast forward, and even block any content that hints at advertising. As far as Millennials are concerned, traditional marketing campaigns are considered impersonal and lack real substance. Consumers no longer rely merely on advertisements and word-of-mouth; they have tools necessary to find the product or service best fit for them. Marketers must change their approach to not only be catchy and desirable, but also to convince the new generation of consumers they are the most valuable choice among all others out there. There is now a need for marketers to be acutely aware of how their consumers are compiling information when making a purchasing decision, and how to capitalize on this newfound obstacle and turn it into an opportunity.[17]

Brands can no longer rely on pushing out products to whoever will listen anymore. Traditional advertising is no longer as relevant as

---

[16] Lauren Friedman, 'Millennials And the Digital Experience: Getting Your Digital Act Together', *Forbes*, (8 February 2017) https://www.forbes.com/sites/laurenfriedman/2017/02/08/millennials-and-the-digital-experience-getting-your-digital-act-together/?sh=40e666f5730d]

[17] Brian Hunter, 'Push vs. Pull marketing: How millennials are changing the game', *CorporateInk*, (1 May 2017) https://corporateink.com/push-pull-marketing-millennials/

it used to be. Today, online paid-for streaming services are popular not only for their ease and efficiency, but also because they are ad-free. This generation is inundated with advertising, which has made it easier to simply ignore due to the sheer volume of it. Not only are they learning to tune out, they're even paying extra to not experience it. Very few brands win over Millennials with creative, emotive and innovative ads. In a marketing centric world, brands have to master the art of digital experiences. However, being creative, innovative or emotive doesn't come naturally to every business. 'Pull' marketing, however, is relatively new and increasingly popular in the Web 2.0 world. A pull campaign focuses on swaying customers in your direction. It occurs when potential customers go out and actively search for information on a product or service, comparing and contrasting different providers to find the best deal or fit for themselves. Pull marketing is quickly emerging as the clear optimal strategy as the public's perception and reception of advertising evolves. People's reaction to push marketing is growing more unfavourable, and pull marketing is capitalizing on the fact that people don't like to be aggressively sold to. It is unfortunate that many firms have not yet awakened to this new pull-marketing, brand-centric reality.

According to a recent Nielsen study, Millennials want to be more informed about companies, their products, and their business practices. Millennials also report that they like hearing from a brand when the communication is not about selling a product; they want to feel like brands are building a relationship with them as an individual, not just as a consumer. What's the difference? Talk to them and talk with them instead of talking 'at them'. Inbound marketing employs the development of strategic digital assets such as blog posts, videos, eBooks, white papers, etc. to share relevant and timely content with your target audience. It uses people's own interests to motivate customers to search them out. This often embodies itself in a brand building as much expertise in their craft as possible. When a company posts valuable content about their area of expertise on a social media site, it's more credible than when a company posts an advertisement on traditional media. Consumers are drawn to the company that has branded itself as the expert. 71 per cent of consumers who have a good social media service experience with a brand are likely to recommend it to others. This high rate of referral is evidence that social media is a very effective way for a company to spread their message. This focus doesn't have to be directly related to the product or service at hand either. Companies that embrace pull marketing are using causes, values, and social responsibility to differentiate themselves from their competition.

Comparing this to traditional ad campaigns, which are more of a broadcast, inbound marketing takes a more organic, non-interruptive, and personalized approach to gain your customer's attention. Millennials consume media differently than their older counterparts, exercising greater control over when and where they watch, listen, and read content, and on which device. While an integrated, multi-channel approach is best across all generations, it carries even more weight when reaching Millennials.[18]

Even the sponsored content on social media, which is considered the better option to raise awareness and brand recognition, is not considered trustworthy. This is where the 'pull' aspect really comes into play. Someone might see or recognize a brand through advertisements, but the internet provides us with a resource to see if it's really great, affordable, or valuable as the advertisement claims it to be. More often than not, it's not. There's only so much marketers can do through advertising a product or service. At the end of the day, it is the quality and service of the brand that comes across as the most authentic. It remains as the most powerful hook to potential consumers. Once marketers obtain awareness from their target market, they have to continue to impress them by ensuring they are the best product out there for their consumer base. This is no doubt challenging for marketers and brands, but it is the best way for them to continuously adapt in this new age.

Now it might seem like all of the above mistakes are common sense in this day and age and yet, you will be surprised to notice the

---

[18] 'Marketing to Millennials in Digital Age', *TopRight*, (13 October 2016) https://www.toprightpartners.com/insights/marketing-millennials-digital-age/

number of small businesses, especially family businesses, that are either unprepared or unwilling to make the changes to adapt to the new way of marketing. After all, if it isn't broken, why fix it? I've noticed this mentality amongst many family businesses because let's face it, doing anything new is always harder before it gets easier. Most business owners who have been around for decades tend to feel that the new technologies are more trouble than they're really worth. They've been doing well for so long and they've connected really well with their existing customer base, so they don't see the threat. Acquiring the skills, resources, and time to manage a mobile app, create content and engage with consumers on social media seems like more work, and it is! It is normal for anyone to feel a little intimidated with all the options and opportunities to revamp their marketing strategies. Unfortunately, choosing to avoid technology that was designed to make your life easier will only help your competition to gain more market share. That is why it is crucial to lean in to the younger generation, understand their behaviours really well so that you can insulate your business from all kinds of disruptions.

Mistake #6: Not Knowing Your Audience Better Than They Know Themselves.

It's a known fact that this generation of young adults view the world and your brand experiences differently than other generations. This group is also changing the way all other generations are interacting with technology, with brands, and even with one another. So the question you should be asking yourself is, *Why aren't you already studying them?* The good news is, you've already picked up this book, so you're on the right track. :)

If you are looking to target Millennials as your primary consumer group, it only makes sense that you get to understand them better than they understand themselves. That means going beyond the typical stereotypes you read about them in the media and really having in-depth conversations with this group. What we typically find about Millennials through Google is merely the tip of the iceberg. Dive a little deeper and we get to see beyond the fluff. As the saying goes, get a PhD in your customer's mindset and you will be able to make a lot more sales than you could ever imagine. What you should have on your mind is, how to effectively and efficiently market to Millennials. More research dollars are to this group because of their purchase power. The historical relationship between brands and consumers has been transactional. Consumers bought products to fulfil a specific need, while brands sold goods in exchange for money.

Today, brands have to navigate a new dimension. Millennial consumers are buying products based on values and beliefs. In an age when most products perform the same function, people want to know the brand story and its impact on society. Companies need to connect with new audiences to build brand loyalty and lifetime customer value. Young people want to know where brands stand on causes that matter the most to them. It's crucial for brands to conduct in-depth research on emerging audiences to determine the pace of change required. Gucci has started accepting cryptocurrencies to appeal to the young adults while Pandora has launched a sustainable lab-grown diamond collection. Our future customers are so different from our past and present customers that we have to design different experiences for them. We need to figure out how they operate because it is very different from even five years ago.

Here's a fun quiz for you to check your understanding of this group. What do the following words mean? Try to answer these without asking anyone or googling for the answer.

- Salty
- Receipts
- Canceled
- NGL
- Thirst trap
- Glow up
- On fleek
- Swol
- Sus
- Clap back
- Flex

- Ghosted
- Squad
- No Cap
- Shade

For brands that want to successfully reach Millennials, they need to speak their language. They perk up when hearing or reading words that could have come from the mouths of their peers, as these messages warrant comfort and trust. As a brand, if you don't understand the Millennial generation, it can mean the difference between your business growing, or its slow and painful death. If you want your business to stand out and take a share of the big bucks that Millennials are prepared to spend, your marketing campaigns and strategies have to speak to their specific characteristics and target their needs. Millennials as kids, were glued to Game Boys, Playstations, and Sega Mega Drives. The internet helped them with their school work and it is the computer lab in schools where they connected with their classmates and played online games like Neopets while the teacher was teaching. In that process of interacting with one another online, they created a new language of their own. It includes acronyms, abbreviations, punctuation lapses, and a new type of shorthand. If you don't get it, your brand won't have a voice.

Millennials want to feel connected and involved when it comes to their purchases, and traditional marketing does not encourage this. Outbound marketing methods, like magazine ads, direct mail campaigns, and radio spots, do not impress Millennials. In the mind of a young consumer, these campaigns are impersonal and company-focused, filled with logos and void of any real substance. This generation demands more customer-driven, personalized marketing. Only 1 per cent of Millennials say a compelling advertisement can build trust. Hard sell won't sell. That's why these young consumers do a lot of their research via blogs, forums, and YouTube videos. Odds are that an intrusive ad isn't going to be a deciding factor. While such ads may be relevant to the person's search history and may put the idea in their head, seeing it wasn't their choice. Millennials feel empowered to make their own online choices, which are usually inspired by their peers or other authentic content. When you offer your audience content they would proudly share with others, you're building a real brand–consumer relationship.

As mentioned before, Millennials are a value-based generation in that they need to know: What's in it for me? Why should I choose your brand over all other brands? As a brand, it's important that you showcase how your product, service and company supports this generations' key values. Research from Nielsen supports this and shows that Millennials will often pay more for brands that support green initiatives or have local roots. Putting their money where their hearts are, makes it increasingly important to sell the 'why' of your company.

Think about It

- What marketing mistakes have you noticed in your own business (if any)?
- How has marketing changed over the years for you?
- How can you leverage this generation to get more clients?
- Which of the new words were you familiar with?
- How important is it for you to understand the lingo and the context of the Millennial generation in order to market to them effectively?

Chapter 3

Behavioural Psychology of the Millennial Consumer: A Deep Dive

Marketing X Technology X Generations

The fundamentals of marketing and advertising are thousands of years old. In the book *Quantum Marketing*, Raja Rajamannar mentions a practice from ancient China, where candy makers played the bamboo flute to attract customers. That was sonic branding in ancient times to attract customers. Marketing is a relatively recent phenomenon that really began prior to the twentieth century and it has never stopped evolving from its simple beginnings. In the early nineteenth century, a woman who wanted a new dress only had two choices. Either she has to make her own dress or she has to hire someone to make one for her. If she decided to hire someone, she had the responsibility of picking out the fabric, getting it measured, and the dress would be custom-made to her proportions. Prior to the industrial revolution, people made most of what they consumed. Any excess household production could be brought to town and sold or traded for other goods. This type of economy is what we know as subsistence economy. In a pure subsistence economy, there is hardly any need for marketing to facilitate any exchanges because each household produces what it consumes.

With the advent of the industrial revolution, however, the producers of many types of goods were not households but businesses. When the producers of products are not the consumers of those products, exchanges must take place.

The biggest leap in marketing happened with the advent of the printing press from the fifteenth century. Producers of goods used to stamp their products with their signature mark. This is seen as the earliest form of the logo to signal to buyers on who created the product. It reminded consumers that specific products came from specific vendors and merchants and that they could return to that vendor for the same kind of goods with the same level of quality. Then as Johannes Gutenberg invented the printing press, mass production of these symbols on many forms of paper medium became possible. This gave birth to the earliest form of print advertising. Advertisements appeared in magazines and posters. Product packaging started incorporating features and benefits. In the industrial age, it was a challenge to manufacture a product. However, it was relatively easy to sell it. Something as basic as a pair of scissors required hundreds of works, a plant and the right equipment to produce at scale. Once they were made though, people flocked to buy them. The real challenge back then was keeping up with the demand. The term 'gross domestic product' comes from this era because people measured the economy based on how much could be produced. It was pretty much assumed that if it could be made, it could be sold. People who could create made a fortune back in the day. This was known as the production era because the main priority of many companies was the reduction of the cost of production.

Companies believed that exchanges could be facilitated merely by lowering manufacturing costs, and in turn, pass along the cost savings to customers in the form of lower prices. When Henry Ford implemented the assembly line, the focus on production and more efficient work principles took center stage. Reduced production costs can lead to reduced selling prices and thus appeal to the largest segment of customers. Unfortunately, due to the First World War and the Second World War, the turbulent economic conditions associated with the late 1920s through 1940s caused many companies to fail. As a result, companies looked for other ways to facilitate the exchange process.

This brought about the sales era, because many companies' main priority was to get rid of or move their products out of the factory door using a variety of selling techniques. During the sales era, companies believed that they could enhance their sales by using a variety of promotional techniques designed to inform and persuade customers to buy their products. Marketing had a literal, rational, and completely product-centric paradigm back then. The presumption was that consumers made their purchase decisions logically and rationally. If you produced the best product, you automatically attracted consumers. Thus, the marketing strategy back then was pure and simple: Beat the competition and make sure the consumers know about it. They leveraged the product's feature set that was different from and better than the competition. With the mass production came a level of commoditization and a level of product parity.

Brands started focusing on superiority in product quality which resulted in marginal differentiation and minimal competitive advantage at best. Some brands even started exaggerating features by getting credible or good-looking people to endorse the brands to make consumers believe the claims. As a result, consumers started losing trust over brands and advertisements slowly started losing their credibility. Here's the caveat: It's worth noting that the use of attractive models in advertising is not inherently bad or unethical. However, when brands rely solely on physical appearance to sell products, or when they reinforce narrow beauty standards that exclude people who don't fit those standards, it can become problematic. Virginia Slims was a brand of cigarettes marketed exclusively to women, and the brand's advertising campaigns from the 1960s through the 1990s often featured slender, glamorous models smoking cigarettes. The ads used slogans like 'You've come a long way, baby' to suggest that smoking was a symbol of women's liberation and independence. GoDaddy as a web hosting and domain registration company gained notoriety for its use of attractive models in its SuperBowl commercials and they were criticized for objectifying women and reinforcing gender stereotypes.

Until the early 1800s, people mainly bought products based on what they needed. They would experience some kind of pain, and they would search for a solution to solve it. For instance, food. When the cavemen needed food, they would search for it, kill it, and bring it home. Today, we do the same thing by ordering it online. In 1886, the Yellow Pages directory was created and it helped consumers find exactly what they needed. Except, for business owners, you had to wait for someone to contact you. They had to wait for consumers to experience the pain in order for them to search for you. When the television was invented in 1927, the shift from search advertising (like Yellow Pages) to interruption advertising began. People who watched TV were not in search of new products, but as they got exposed to different commercials, it placed a seed of desire in their hearts and minds. It no longer became a thing about needs. It was about what you wanted. Marketers realized that the TV commercial gave them a window to plant the seed of desire and show the perceived value of their products and services. As long as you had a captive audience, you can engage them through entertainment or education and create desire for what you sold. Interruption advertising happens all around us today. This is very similar to the vacuum cleaner salesperson or water-filter salesperson that still knocks our doors today—unannounced.

The nineteenth century gave birth to ad agencies and ads for soaps. After that, we saw radio, newspapers, television, cable, and the internet come along. Fun fact: The first radio ad hit the airwaves in 1922. AT&T paid a total of $100 for a ten-minute advertisement to promote Long Island apartments. By 1930, nearly 90 per cent of all radio stations in the US were broadcasting radio ads. By 1941, all of those radio ad spots were replaced with TV ad spots. The 1940s, 1950s and 1960s made way to a simpler, more family-friendly style of TV advertising. Brightly designed visuals were a magical experience in the golden age of colour television.

Searching vs Scrolling

After the TV dominated the marketing scene for decades, it got disrupted by the internet and data-based marketing. When the internet started, we can see the same patterns as we did in TV commercial marketing. People had some type of need, and they would immediately head over to the search engines to look for a solution to their problems. It was mostly search-based in the early stages of the internet until social media came along. As the internet disrupted TV and print media marketing, a new platform emerged not too long after to disrupt marketing once again. Facebook, as it was known then, spiked from fifty users to a hundred million users in a short span of time. This kickstarted the social media marketing tsunami that enveloped the world within a few years. In 2007, Facebook announced the first-ever social interruption advertising with Facebook Ads. As people were scrolling, your ads would show up on their Facebook feed. It worked in the same manner as the TV advertisements. People would be online stalking their friends and your ad would show up in their feed. In order for your ad to be effective, it needed to speak directly to the desires of your consumers. The concept is the same. Interrupt and intrigue them to learn more by getting in touch. The copy and the creative for the ad have to be well thought out for this strategy to be effective.

According to a global overview conducted in January of 2022, more than half of the world (58.4 per cent) now utilizes social media, with 424 million new users joining the action within the last twelve months. When you come to think of it, the marketing world was so different just twenty years ago i.e. early 2000s, where advertising typically happened on TV, radio, print, and billboards. The exponential growth of users is directly correlated to the birth and growth of social media marketing. This is the place where consumers and businesses have discovered the golden opportunity to engage, network, and grow together with content. Here's how Millennials feel about the different platforms.

TikTok: TikTok has emerged as a hugely popular platform among Millennials in recent years. The platform's short-form videos and algorithmic recommendations have made it a favourite for entertainment and creative expression. It's worth noting that the platform has exploded in popularity among Millennials and younger users in recent years. Many Millennials use TikTok for entertainment and creative expression, and the platform has become a major force in shaping internet culture.

Instagram: Instagram is very popular among Millennials, who tend to use it as a platform for sharing photos and videos with their friends and followers. Many Millennials also use Instagram to follow influencers and brands that align with their interests and values.

LinkedIn: LinkedIn is a professional networking platform that many Millennials use to connect with other professionals and job opportunities. While it may not be as popular among younger Millennials as other platforms, it can be a useful tool for building a professional network.

YouTube: YouTube is very popular among Millennials, who use it to watch a wide variety of videos, from educational content to entertainment. Many Millennials also use the platform to follow their favourite creators and personalities.

Snapchat: Snapchat was once a very popular platform among Millennials, but its popularity has declined somewhat in recent years. However, many Millennials still use Snapchat for sharing ephemeral content with their friends, and the platform's filters and lenses remain popular.

Twitter: Twitter has a somewhat mixed reputation among Millennials. While some use it as a platform for engaging in political discourse and following news events, others find it to be a toxic and exhausting environment.

Pinterest: While Pinterest is not as widely used among Millennials as some other platforms, it does have a devoted following among those who enjoy DIY projects, home decor, and fashion. Many Millennials also use Pinterest for inspiration and planning purposes

Reddit: Reddit is a social news aggregation and discussion platform that has gained a cult following among Millennials. Many use the platform to participate in niche communities and discussion forums related to their interests.

Facebook: While Facebook was once the dominant social media platform among Millennials, many younger users have since moved on to other platforms. However, some Millennials still use Facebook to stay in touch with friends and family members, and to participate in interest-based groups.

The chances of a business being seen while marketing through these platforms, grows immensely. While previously you may have posted your advertisement on a billboard or in the newspaper in hopes that an interested party may eventually stumble across it, social media helps to provide an invaluable shortcut to what was previously a luck-based process. Algorithms in these platforms are trained to recognize and categorize the interests of individuals on the platform. This helps marketers to better target the right group of their products and services. In other words, the products being recommended by the algorithm on social media are more likely to appeal to the viewer since it usually has something to do with their interests. Furthermore, since social media usually allows for the sharing and re-sharing of content, it allows the advertisement to be spread more quickly and much further than traditional means of advertising usually allow. This allows marketers to reach their intended customer base faster and more efficiently.

Taylor Swift built her brand using MySpace (remember the OG social media account?) by fostering one-to-one connection with her fans. She was constantly communicating with them by responding to comments, signing autographs, and taking photos with them. She started her internet presence early on and did fan-outreach through MySpace.

Another example is actress Sophie Turner (best known for her role as Sansa Stark on the HBO series *Game of Thrones*), who admits that she was chosen for a role over another actress that she considered 'far better' than her because she had a bigger social media following.

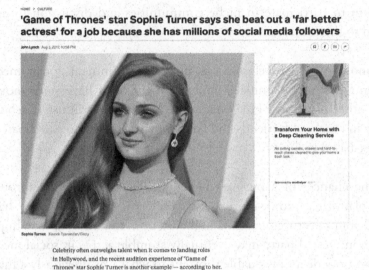

HOME > CULTURE

'Game of Thrones' star Sophie Turner says she beat out a 'far better actress' for a job because she has millions of social media followers

John Lynch Aug 3, 2017, 10:58 PM

Transform Your Home with a Deep Cleaning Service

No puting corners, unseen and hard-to-reach places cleaned to give your home a fresh look.

Sponsored by seethelper

Sophie Turner. Kevork Djansezian/Getty

Celebrity often outweighs talent when it comes to landing roles
in Hollywood, and the recent audition experience of "Game of
Thrones" star Sophie Turner is another example — according to her.

[Source: https://www.insider.com/game-of-thrones-star-sophie-turner-says-she-got-role-due-to-social-media-following-2017-8]

> 'A lot of what I have achieved is about timing and luck, but it is also,
> and I hate to say it, about a big social-media following,'
>
> —Sophie Turner

The numbers you have on social media can impress people who don't look beneath the surface. Even traditional book publishers give more attention and priority to authors with a substantial social media following compared to those without it.

With engagement, promotions, branding, and working with the algorithm, social media is a great way to rack up views, get your products noticed, and encourage consumers to make a purchase. Social media marketing has altered the way people and companies interact— from customer service, product development, advertising, PR, and more. In the past, many were hesitant to call a brand and disclaim their unsatisfactory experience, or even share a positive one. With the help of social media, businesses can connect with their customers like a friend who understands their needs and suggests useful products.

Through social media ads, businesses now have the ability to capture data instead of making wild, uneducated guesses of what their customers would really like. Based on the customers who bought the product or responded to the ad, they can dive deeper into the psychology of the customer and identify their income, buying habits, preferences, dislikes, needs and wants etc.

To compound on the effect of social media platforms, the first iPhone, was released on 29 June 2007. Mobile phones and mobile devices completely altered the consumer landscape for once and for all. The smartphone today is seen as an extension of the body with consumers going to bed and waking up with it. This is where we are at in terms of marketing. Technology has evolved through multiple cycles and has had a direct impact on consumer behaviours. With exponential increases in processing power, as the miniaturization of components and devices happened, plus the availability of affordable internet and the big leap in user interface, we saw the birth of mobile smart phones that transformed the marketing landscape once again.

Also known as the next major technological disruption for marketing, everything about marketing, advertising and media changed in an instant. It became an inflection point at which speed, scale and impact was born and nothing about marketing has been the same since. Big companies started realizing the value of becoming a media business by creating content and flooding it online. They realized that it was no longer a toy or something that teenagers played with. It was something that all businesses around the world would have to get their head around and actively engage with. The big companies kicked it off, and today even the tiny businesses have jumped on the social media bandwagon. Similarly, we are observing a new trend around data. The new focus became using data to create more targeted marketing which minimized waste, stretched the dollar and vastly improved the company's ROI. Marketers gained an extraordinary ability to reach, communicate to, and impress their prospects and customers as never before—at scale, with economy and precision.

Highly individualized marketing messages that were customized, memorable and impactful became the norm. They simply did this through collecting data from their consumers, crunching that data and using the insights from the data collected to craft personalized marketing messages to the masses. For instance, Amazon is creating a personalized shopping experience based on your past shopping habits. Spotify has personalization built into its platform. YouTube too. That's how these platforms know what kind of song or video you will most probably enjoy. Social media platforms, with the newsfeed, is based on a personalization algorithm woven into it. Big companies are discovering more and more ways to deliver personalized, interactive experiences that feel very much like they really understood you as a consumer. The suggestions that are made, based on the data collected, are designed to have a high acceptance rate by the consumer. Just as you can predict your future health based on your eating and exercise habits, so too can a company today with the level of data they have at their disposal.

The new savvy marketers are learning what customers are interested in before pushing ads their way. A little research ahead of time is paying off big time. Targeting became so specific that consumer advocates demanded the regulators to implement the 'Do Not Call or Do Not Mail' lists in the US also known as Personal Data Protection Act (PDPA) in Singapore. At the moment, only huge companies know how to leverage personalization for the masses and win market share through data analytics whereas the smaller companies have to scramble to get their heads around how to capture the right data and glean powerful insights from it in order to personalize their marketing messages. More than 70 per cent of consumers are more than happy to give away relevant data if it leads to personalized recommendations and 90 per cent of young consumers willingly give their data for a personalized experience. It's a win-win for both parties—companies get the data they need and consumers get exactly what they are after without having to look hard for it. Young consumers even feel annoyed when there isn't any personalization. They feel angry when the website doesn't remember that they already bought that product and recommends it again to them. And I believe it is going to get more complex as we go into the future.

According to Hosain Rahman, CEO of Jawbone, the thermostat in your office cabin should know a) who you are and b) are you feeling hot or cold. Today, it doesn't know that, no matter how smart it is.

It doesn't know if you're hot because you're sick, or because you went out for a run or simply because it is really hot outside. It should have the ability to know those things to trigger the right response. Your car should know if you're tired, are you alert enough; it should know if you are aware of what is happening, if you have had enough sleep, and it should react to all those data accordingly. All of this can be possible if we get the devices we wear, also known as wearables, smart enough to interact with other devices. For instance, getting your smartwatch to interact with your smart car to let it know you are tired, feeling feverish and lethargic. We are going to slowly transition from the 'Internet of Things' to the 'Internet of You', where these devices are in service to make your life better. Very soon, devices will identify the temperature that you sleep fastest at and will automatically change the temperature as it approaches your sleeping time. The precision and personalization that is available with data changes the nature of marketing and advertising. It is easy to imagine gyms seeking new clients by targeting those who have shown search interest in getting fitter, enabled by online tracking or shoe retailers marketing to individuals who wear step-counting devices to hit 10,000 steps a day.

There's a common saying about Facebook,

'We are not the customers of Facebook, we are the product. Facebook is selling us to advertisers.'

However, with the 'Internet of You', users may find they are both the customer who purchased a product and the target of a secondary customer (an advertiser) who bought their data. Google highlighted that the biggest issue in this new world is trust. Companies must find ways to reassure consumers and position their brands as trustworthy.

To build trust amongst Millennials, you must first understand their lives, digital habits, struggles, role models, cultural touchstones, how they manage 'Fear of Missing Out' (FOMO) and figuring out where they fit into a rapidly changing world. However, most of what sets this generation apart is an unrelenting relationship with information, media consumption, and mobile technology. In any relationship, it is important to really listen and understand the requirements of the other party. In order to market and sell more to Millennials, brands have to listen hard. Over the past few years, I have conducted hundreds of interviews with Millennials and distilled my findings into a detailed list of Millennial attributes and preferences.

Preference #1: Transparency

'Transparency is key when marketing to Millennials. This generation has virtually any information they can imagine at their fingertips and are constantly being bombarded with messages. Being able to cut through that noise and meet them where they are through a variety of mediums is vital. Whether it's how we share our information about the ingredients and the testing of our products, to the use of user generated content, keeping things simple, real, and honest is how we market to all of our consumers, but is especially important to the Millennial who craves that messaging and holistic experience . . .'

—Jane Iredale, founder and CEO of Iredale Mineral
Cosmetics, LLC, a wellness brand crafting clean,
cruelty-free makeup with skin care benefits[19]

With modern media, information spreads more quickly than ever before, and scandalous news about a business travels at lightning speeds. Companies that aren't transparent will be found out. There's no question about it. It is impossible to hide the truth, so don't bother trying. Covering up is not a fix. With a few swipes on their phone, this generation has the ability to obtain any information within seconds. Millennials grew up at a time where they had access to computers and smartphones during their childhood to teenage years. With the internet easily accessible on a mobile device, they had the technology readily available to search for answers through Google. That's when websites became the craze. But what the internet did is give the consumer the power to question brands who mask certain information that is important for the consumer to know before making a purchase. Many

---

[19] Iredale, J. '27 expert tips for marketing to millennials', *inc.com*, (2017), https://www.inc.com/christina-desmarais/27-expert-tips-for-marketing-to-millennials.html

companies have used insidious marketing strategies to programme individuals since they were young, as a child, to crave, desire and want things they want you to buy.

For instance, the Milo drink powder can have a sportsman on the cover and is marketed as something that actually makes you healthy. However, when you look at the ingredients, it shows 9.3 grams of sugar for every 20 grams of a serving, which amounts to around 46.5 per cent sugar. Yet, it is promoted as a health drink. Even the TV ad played in the Philippines had an invented disease, termed the 'energy gap' that four out of five students suffer from. It's no wonder people have trust issues with advertisements.[20]

There are countless companies that do this. They omit key information or mask them to enhance their sales. Nutella and Ferrero Rocher have been sued for portraying chocolate as breakfast. In fact, according to Vishen, Nutella—which is sold as chocolate—isn't even real chocolate. It is primarily palm oil. Out of 15 grams of a serving, 8.4 grams of it is—you've guessed it—sugar. Companies like these are often coming up with new ways to label sugar. Companies are using different names for sugar in their packaging to confuse you. Did you know that these are all the terms that basically mean sugar?

- Agave syrup
- Barley Malt syrup
- Brown rice syrup
- Carob syrup
- Corn syrup
- Golden syrup
- Malt syrup
- Maple syrup
- Sorghum syrup
- Sugar beet syrup

Millennials are inherently distrustful, especially of large organizations. Companies need to open the door and build positive

---

[20] https://www.youtube.com/watch?v=zDgmUtO8aUA

relationships with them to get in touch with them in reality. In order to do that, they need to show them exactly what the brand is about. Honesty and being transparent can only come from one value: striving to deliver the best possible outcome to your customers. If your brand values are focused on profit over people, it is going to backfire on the brand. This applies even to how the company takes care of their employees and their community, and encourages their success.

> 'Millennials are looking for transparency in the way of clean and understandable ingredient panels and companies that display social and environmental responsibility. Millennials want to feel like their buying decisions are making an impact both in their life and the lives of others. Carrington Farm's products all have clear labels laying out the ingredients and their uses in each of the products. Our products are available in mainstream grocery as well as natural stores so they are easy to find for almost everyone.'
> —Debbie Shandel, EVP and CMO of health
> food company Carrington Company[21]

Domino's Pizza launched a campaign in which it took a brave decision to address the dissatisfaction of its customers around the quality of its product. Patrick Doyle, Domino's president back then, spoke candidly about the lack of love consumers had for the company. Domino's documented the comments on online forums, blog posts, tweets that said 'Mass produced, boring, bland pizza' and actually aired that footage. Footage from real focus groups where customers said things like 'Doesn't feel like there's much love in Domino's pizza' and 'Domino's pizza crust, to me, is like cardboard' was also shared. The videos also encapsulated employee reactions, with their dejected expressions and emotions where they said 'It hurts' and 'That hits you right in the heart'. When many companies try to hide criticism, Domino's embraced it and broadcasted it. They took responsibility

---

[21] Iredale, J. '27 expert tips for marketing to millennials', *inc.com*, (2017), https://www.inc.com/christina-desmarais/27-expert-tips-for-marketing-to-millennials.html

and showcased the extensive measures it was taking to get back on track to regain customer's respect. As a result, in their next quarter's financial results, the company proved that its transparency paid off.[22]

Millennials have gotten smarter with the internet and despise brands that conceal important information that should be declared with regards to their products. Instead of merely window shopping to learn more about products and services from the salesperson, they started going on Google to find the same answers. Over time, it has become the default practice. Millennials want to know you before they can trust you. They will read reviews and testimonials on your website, but they will put more importance on the reviews from independent sources or blogs. One of the best examples you can find is Tripadvisor. com, a website where millions of people share the knowledge and opinions about the travel space for free. Companies that are caught omitting key information tend to experience a backlash when they get exposed. Patagonia, a company loved by many Millennials for being transparent, shares its 'environmental dirty laundry'. The company uses the 'Footprint chronicles' section of its website to allow consumers to see the environmental impact of its various products. In their website, they say, 'The goal is to use transparency about our supply chain to help us reduce our adverse social and environmental impacts—and on an industrial scale.' Instead of bragging about how great and how ecofriendly the company is, Patagonia is openly showing what it is doing and expressing what it would like to do better.[23]

Transparency is quickly becoming a strong differentiator because Millennials trust their peers and independent experts more than they trust the company. They want to find impartial, honest, and sincere evaluations from people in their community. This is why referrals from

---

[22] Luke LaBree, 'Domino's Pizza has managed to pull off a huge turnaround; in part by listening and responding to their customers in a uniquely-honest PR advertising blitz', *Dennis*. https://dennisfoodservice.com/dominos-pizza-turnaround-case-study/

[23] Dave Kerpen, *Likeable Business: Why Today's Consumers Demand More And How Leaders Can Deliver*, (Mc-Graw Hill Professional, 16 December 2012)

influencers are becoming more powerful than advertising. There is
a caveat though. Millennials only trust influencers who are genuine
over the long term i.e. influencers who truly endorse the products
themselves. Like all things, over time, people can tell if the influencer
genuinely likes the product and services or simply marketed it because
the company paid them well. That's why the more transparent the
influencers are, the more trust they have with their audiences. In the
same vein, the more you endorse products purely for profits, the lesser
Millennials tend to trust them. Bold claims and flashy marketing-speak
won't earn you as many points as it might with other generations.

Marketing has evolved a fair bit over time. Along the way,
marketing swung full in on emotions when marketers realized
people make decisions emotionally more than they do rationally or
logically. A study published in the Journal of Consumer Research
found that emotions can have a powerful impact on how consumers
perceive brands and make purchasing decisions. Many marketers have
embraced the idea that emotional connections with customers are
crucial to building strong, long-lasting relationships with them. This
has led to a shift in marketing strategies towards creating emotionally
resonant content and experiences that can establish a connection with
customers. We see this with the rise of influencer marketing that relies
heavily on creating emotional connections between influencers and
their audiences. Brands have even started using storytelling to create
emotional connections with their customers purely based on the aim of
building brand loyalty.[24]

That generated ad campaigns that were focusing on incorporating
emotions completely. As TV entered the marketing scene, stories
were told powerfully through the visual and audio media? to generate
emotion. What's even more interesting is that a lot of the emotional
claims lacked scientific and data-backed proof. As marketing leaned
towards emotions, it became more about the experience than it was
about moving goods off shelves. Marketing started to mine emotions.

---

[24] M.F. Luce, J.W. Payne, & Bettman, J. R., 'Emotional Trade-off Difficulty
And Choice', *Journal of Consumer Research*, (2001), 27(3), 329-34

Brands and companies began creating emotional spaces and then occupying those spaces because of one key reason: Product features could be matched or bettered which dislodges the market position of the product. Coca-Cola associated itself with happiness, Apple with thinking differently, and Nike with overcoming adversity.

However, once a product occupies an emotional territory, the brand pretty much owns that territory for good. In order to capture the hearts of the consumers, brands started focusing on methods that associated their brand with emotions. Consumer mindsets, motivations, attitudes, and behaviour became the focus of marketers. This kickstarted attitudinal metrics, usage and habits studies, focus groups and psychographic research. The more marketers learnt about their consumer's role models and aspirations, they started looking out for celebrities as a way to bridge the emotional gap. From 1954 to 1999, the cowboy aesthetic became the face of Marlboro cigarettes. Connecting smoking with cowboys made cigarette smoking a lot cooler. It tied smoking with the image of freedom, independence and masculinity. It became a sign of adulthood. Hollywood also played a role in promoting cigarettes. Tobacco companies partnered with movie producers and actors to get them to hold cigarettes in the hands of revered actors and stars. It became evident to consumers that not all partnerships may be authentic; celebrities are more than happy to endorse products and services they don't believe in if the financials make sense. That's why it is important for brands to build an authentic brand for themselves to win over the trust of the Millennials.

Preference #2: Authenticity

'They can spot an ad from a million miles away. They are keenly aware of what is marketing speak versus real talk. So keep your communications, advertisements, and content as authentic as possible. Provide real, actionable tips, be transparent in sharing your company values and keep adjectives to a minimum. Above all else, know your authentic voice and use it effectively to connect, not just market to them.'

—Mahesh Chaddah, co-founder of Reservations.com

In January 2023, Zoe Gabriel, seventeen, was mocked by some users after she uploaded a video on TikTok, thanking her father for her 'first luxury bag' from Charles & Keith. That one video prompted an onslaught of hate simply because she considered the brand a luxury one. Charles & Keith was founded by siblings Charles & Keith in 1996, who learnt the ropes by working at their mother's store in Singapore. It morphed into a household name very quickly with more than 600 stores employing over 4000 employees worldwide.

The Charles & Keith tote bag is priced at SGD $79.90 on their website and it is the most expensive bag she owns. So why was Zoe mocked on TikTok?? Probably because some users might not consider the Charles & Keith brand to be a luxury brand, compared to others out in the market. It was a traumatizing experience for Zoe but she impressed many when she replied to trolls by posting a follow up video where she tearily explained her humble background and talked about privilege.

You probably can guess what happened next.

Both her clips have since gone viral, attracting a total of 8.5 million views. Then, Charles & Keith reached out to Zoe after viewing her clip. The company spokesman said, 'Our hearts really went out to Zoe, but we were so impressed with how gracefully she handled the situation, displaying wisdom far beyond her years and values that resonated with us greatly.'

Zoe and her father were invited to have lunch with the founders who also came from humble beginnings and were given an exclusive behind-the-scenes company tour at their headquarters. The latest news as of March 2023, Zoe was spotted posing with the brand's Alia bag. Zoe made the ultimate clap back by responding well to hate online and Charles & Keith increased its brand awareness through this sage by empowering Zoe as a brand community ambassador. Netizens applauded the move as a win for the right values. This is authenticity in action.

Marketing used to be heavily focused on what we said about products. If a company put a great advertisement in a print publication, they would often get an increase in sales. Millennials don't care about the catchy phrases or features used to describe products. They crave to engage with an authentic brand voice. It would have never been acceptable amongst the previous generations for companies to speak out on political stances or social justice, but these two things can actually help you connect more with these consumers. If your values align with a customer's, they are more inclined to support your company and buy your products. Authenticity works with every age group, Millennials simply rate it as an even higher priority than Baby Boomers or Gen Xers.

About seven in ten Millennials consider the brand when they make a purchase, which is higher than the five out of ten that is average. This means today's brands have to not only be conscious of their image, they need to be creating messaging that resonates with Millennials. Baby Boomers listening to your YouTube ad might not resonate as much with brand messaging that touches on core values like sustainability and environmental impact, you can be sure that Millennials are listening.

But, how does one really identify an authentic brand? In a world where brands are fighting for consumers and their attention, it is easy for us to get lost in the ways we approach our consumers. Brands that build strong relationships with Millennials have learnt to have their own distinguished voice. You can't build a strong relationship by creating an account on Instagram and expect to connect to the Millennial generation. You have to work at building a relationship. Millennials came of age in an ever-complicated digital environment and have grown adept at tuning out online sales pitches and slogans. Younger generations are turning away from shallow ad claims in favour of relatable human experiences and personalized recommendations. Whether on the phone, in person, or online, Millennials say that dealing with a company should feel consistent. The brand has to establish a true identity that runs through everything they do. More importantly, Millennials need to feel authenticity throughout the digital experience. The question that runs through everyone's mind is this:

Are you doing this to earn my money or are you doing this because you really believe in adding value to me/in this cause?

Starbucks believes in building a company with soul by committing to never stop pursuing the perfect cup of coffee. However, CEO Howard Schultz once compromised the Starbucks customer experience by putting relentless growth and expansion ahead of quality. In order to achieve record growth, the company made decisions that led to watering down of the Starbucks experience and commoditization of the brand. Schultz admitted and apologized for this mistake in a company wide memo: 'I take full responsibility myself but we desperately need to look into the mirror and realize it's time to get back to the core and make the changes necessary to evoke the heritage, the tradition, and the passion we all have for the true Starbucks experience.'

Millennials spend a lot of time online or using apps, and they are constantly looking for engaging content. They go through websites, blogs, and social media platforms for information and have become really savvy in distinguishing between authentic and inauthentic content. Are you creating content to generate a sale, or are you really invested in your customer's journey? Take celebrity endorsements for instance. How much one trusts a celebrity endorsement in this day and age is questionable because the key motivator behind these endorsements is money. If the financials are right, the celebrity is more than happy to endorse. This is why nano-influencers, who have around a 1000 followers or less, have a higher trust amongst their followers as opposed to celebrities with millions of followers. It is believed that nano influencers are less likely to promote a brand that is inconsistent with their values because they value the relationship with their followers.

'We know this group of consumers likes to see themselves in the media they consume and we take that insight quite literally, focusing on user-generated content to help tell our brand story. On Instagram, our guests use our brand hashtag #strikeitup to submit images and videos of themselves in our centers, for a chance to win gift cards in our ongoing consumer promotion, and we are then able to feature these assets in all of our marketing channels. When your consumer can relate to your content in an authentic way—in this case an honest look into the brand experience—your brand message goes a lot farther.'

—Colie Edison, VP of marketing at Bowlmor
AMF, the largest owner and operator of
bowling venues in the world[25]

Sixty per cent of consumers rated user-generated content (UGC) as the most authentic. They include text, images, or video content created by customers about your business and its products or services. Today's mobile-friendly audience constantly seeks word-of-mouth and online reviews to conduct product research. It follows that any brand willing to put out user-generated content like reviews out front is the brand striving to be authentic. Most importantly, the content isn't created by marketers. Encourage your customers to post photos and videos of your products or services online. This can help you gain the attention of consumers previously unfamiliar with your brand while establishing your brand as one that can be trusted. Doritos did this really well where they hosted a 'Crash the Super Bowl' contest where fans of the brand were encouraged to create a Doritos commercial. The winning submission was then aired during the big game and turned out to be an effective way of advertising its own product through user-generated content.

Relevant, genuine opinions from real people who they can relate to is what Millennials look for. Far too often companies mask their real intentions and jump on trends to do one thing: make more sales. Focusing on generating positive customer feedback will help encourage purchases. Especially when social media is involved, it is better to incorporate customer testimonials to build a positive reputation for your brand. The company Five Guys often shares user-generated content and reviews from happy customers on their timeline. To increase customer feedback, they even reach out to customers who enjoyed their service previously to learn how they can be serviced better. By making it as easy as possible to leave customer reviews, companies enjoy valuable feedback

---

[25] Edison, C, '27 expert tips for marketing to Millennials', https://www.inc.com/christina-desmarais/27-expert-tips-for-marketing-to-millennials.html

that helps improve business. Studies have indicated that reviews are a key part of the buying process for Millennials. They will scour the internet for reviews of the product they are considering to purchase and may not buy it if they don't find any reviews online. That's because Millennials don't readily trust a marketer's effort to sell them anything. They value trust, which is why they frequently seek out the opinions of peers and consult user-generated review sites like Tripadvisor and Yelp. Apple's iPhone had a 'Shot on an iPhone' campaign that worked really well. New iPhone users were encouraged to share their original videos for possible inclusion in the national ad campaign. Not only did it provide Apple with hours of footage demonstrating the quality of their phone's video technology, but it also made users feel they were building something for a larger community. By engaging your Millennial fans and asking for UGC as part of their natural day-to-day, you are both acknowledging their important role in the community and not creating additional work for them. This group already shares so much on social media so capturing a small part of it can help to boost your brand exponentially.

To create authentic content, companies must create content that is engaging, informative, and entertaining. This content should introduce them to the brand or product with a high level of transparency. Authenticity goes hand-in-hand with transparency. Millennials are the generation that started focusing more on ethics from their schooling days compared to the previous generations. To successfully promote your products and services to this group, you must establish brand values and ethics that appeal to them. Then, you have to ensure the messaging incorporates these values throughout the different platforms, channels, and websites to attract more Millennials.

Ultimately, being authentic requires you to act like a legitimate human being. Customers want to feel like they are interacting with a person, not a machine or a cold, soulless company. In order to be warmly accepted by your customers, you must present yourself and your business as human, demonstrating a true personality. A great benefit of being perceived as authentic and human is that you're accepted for who you are and given slack for your faults. Authenticity breeds trust and trust earns sales. Let your fans and followers know that there are human beings on the other side of their screens.

Preference #3: Social Good

'Parents of Millennials want to know a product's features and benefits. Millennials require a second layer. What is your why? How do you impact the world? Lead with your purpose. At our company, we believe in doing everything possible to offer solutions for the health and well-being of others. Sometimes that's through our products, but first and foremost, it's through who we are as people. Philanthropy cannot be a side conversation. In our case, we collaborate with charity: water, a nonprofit organization delivering clean, safe drinking water to people in developing countries. We donate $3 from the sale of our [top] selling product—Eye Authority—to help fund water sources worldwide. But it's not enough to hand off a check every year. We're physically going to build our first funded well, and we'll be making our customers a part of it.'

—Annette Rubin, CEO of HydroPeptide, a
personal care line advancing clean science
and epigenetics-driven formulations[26]

Have you noticed the world becoming more eco-friendly over the years? At least, that's how it would appear to the man on the street. Millennials believe brands should stand for something besides profit and it should clearly display the positive impact they make in the world. This expectation is already moving fast toward a new normal. This has been a rallying cry for Millennials for the longest time and it's not going away anytime soon. In 2018, Patagonia made international news when they donated the entirety of their $10 million corporate tax cut to groups committed to protecting air, land, and water, and finding the solutions to the climate crisis. This is on top of their 1 per cent that

---

[26] Annette Rubin, '27 expert tips for marketing to Millennials', (20 April 2017) https://www.inc.com/christina-desmarais/27-expert-tips-for-marketing-to-millennials.html

they give for the Planet initiative which has been running since 1985. Brands need to think about how they can make an impact, no matter how small you may be. The worst thing you can do is to only worry about business as usual.

The world is in a dire state. With the rising cost of living, sluggish job markets, and sky-high prices in the property market, Millennials are tight on cash. Given these circumstances, many want to patronize and work with companies that are not only customer-oriented, but have socially oriented mission statements. In everything they do, Millennials want to feel like they're helping to build a better world. This holds true across most patterns of Millennial behaviour. They want to make a difference at work, at home, and even when they are shopping. Not only is this generation driving brands to be thoughtful about what they say online, they also want brands to be vocal when it matters. The term 'brand activism' is associated with Millennials because of their typical 'buycott' behaviours when brands do more harm than good i.e they switch to more sustainable, ethical brands when the brands they used to buy from continue with poor practices.

A buycott is a form of economic activism in which consumers support a particular company or product based on its socially responsible or ethical practices. In the same vein, it also means to boycott brands that don't follow corporate social responsibility (CSR) objectives. It exerts pressure on companies that have neglected their CSR to alter their practices. Exercising choice in this way generates incentives for companies to align their practices with the customer's values. Boycotting is all about rewarding those who do the right thing and sending the message across by voting with your wallet.

Instead of boycotting companies or products that consumers perceive to be unethical or harmful, buycotts encourage consumers to actively support companies or products that align with their values. In 2016, Ben & Jerry, the ice cream company announced that it would stop sourcing milk from farms that use genetically modified organisms (GMOs). Many consumers who support the anti-GMO movement began to actively support Ben & Jerry's products. Patagonia is an outdoor clothing company that is known for its environmental activism. Many consumers who are passionate about environmental causes have chosen to support Patagonia by purchasing its products. TOMS Shoes is a company that donates a pair of shoes to a child in need for every pair of shoes that it sells. Many consumers who support charitable causes have chosen to purchase TOMS Shoes products as a way to support the company's philanthropic efforts.

In the past, businesses that communicated their values on controversial topics like sustainability, carbon neutral, equality or climate change were deemed high risk. This is because it is easy for companies to come under fire from the public if their actions don't line up with their claims. In 2019, McDonalds introduced paper straws that were non-recyclable. As it is, the practice of cutting down trees to make disposable straws is questionable; now on top of that, those straws are non-recyclable. No wonder it turned out to be a controversy. This is a classic example of a corporate giant pretending to address an issue without actually doing anything. This affects the brand image of the organization and consumers trust the company even less. It undermines the leadership of the organization and is known to affect stock prices of the bigger giants in the market. In such instances, it is safer to not say anything about their work on sustainability than to declare it and come under fire for some inconsistencies that exist within their business.[27]

These topics fall under the category of 'Green Marketing', which is used by companies to build or strengthen their image as ecologically sensitive, but also to spread and make normal new lifestyles and consumption habits that takes into consideration the environment. However, some companies are resorting to 'Greenwashing' instead of 'Green Marketing'. Greenwashing is the act of promoting positive ideals without these ideals actually being a part of the company's values. As per the McDonalds example given above, it involves building a falsified image of the company, often to hide the negative impact it has on the environment. Companies tend to mix up green marketing

---

[27] 'Greenwashing: 11 recent stand-out examples', *Akepa*, (23 July 2021). https://thesustainableagency.com/blog/greenwashing-examples/

with green washing. They think that as long as they jump on the 'green bandwagon', they will establish a better brand presence. Fortunately or unfortunately, it's pretty easy for the consumers of today to see past their actions. It takes consistency to build a company's image and running a campaign for a short period of time doesn't build the kind of goodwill that companies expect to gain when they embrace green initiatives. Green marketing is not a one-off initiative. It should be part of their values, which is reflected in their actions i.e in everything they do as an organization. If the organization is merely talking without any action, Millennials see past it and call them out for it on social media platforms. It boils down to integrity—do you do what you say you will do? Or do you merely provide lip service?

There are four social impact pillars that this generation wants to see brands emphasize:

1. actively invest in improving society and solving social problems
2. prioritize their social impacts
3. be transparent and public about their efforts
4. include their customers in their social endeavours

Millennials know their vote with their wallet makes a difference and they actively seek out brands that have stated their position on some of the hot-button topics today. Today's consumer seeks out like-mindedness in brands which help brands to develop a message that resonates.

In a world where competitive differences are very small, one way brands compete to win the hearts and minds of Millennials is to have a true 'Brand Promise'. Major companies like Starbucks, McDonalds, and KFC were quick to ban plastic straws partly because they saw the opportunity to demonstrate a commitment to sustainability and environmental stewardship. Companies like TOMS Shoes paved the way for charitable companies. Many companies now donate a portion of their profits to a relevant charity, giving consumers a way to directly help while getting something in return. They want to feel their purchasing decisions not only influence their life but the lives of others. Interestingly, this doesn't just apply to the quality of their purchase.

This generation wants their money to support companies who care about giving back to the community.

According to Euclid, 52 per cent of Millennials feel it's important that their values align with the brands they like. If you support a charitable or environmental cause, you are likely to attract Millennial consumers who also support these causes. They demand the best from brands at all times and will happily turn to a competitor if their needs are not met. Provide an opportunity that will let Millennials feel like they're changing the world for the better, and they'll be more likely to support your brand. Being socially conscious, charitable, and environmentally friendly goes far with Millennials. Think how your organization can become a platform that will attract the Millennials. That means standing strongly for a cause that you are passionate about. All it takes is a video that uncovers practices that run counter to a company's messaging to negate years of careful branding.

The social good your brand does must tie in with authenticity, because going at this from a selfish angle will backfire on you.

[Source: https://thesustainableagency.com/blog/greenwashing-examples/]

Another controversy is the greenwashing move by Coca-Cola, which slapped a green label on its drink, 'Coca-Cola Life', to make it appear more healthy or more sustainable. With a 6.6 per cent sugar content, Coca-Cola Life was far from a healthy drink. The more you drink it, the less life you would probably live anyway.

A plastic package containing a new shower curtain is labeled as 'recyclable'. It is not clear whether the package or the shower curtain is recyclable. In either case, the label is deceptive if any part of the package or its contents, excluding minor components, cannot be recycled. Another example is when a trash bag is labeled 'recyclable'. Trash bags are not ordinarily separated from other trash at the landfill or incinerator, so they are highly unlikely to be used again for any purpose. The claim is deceptive because it asserts an environmental benefit where no meaningful benefit exists. Companies are constantly coming up with new and brilliant ways to lie to the man on the street. No wonder people are losing trust over what they claim in their marketing messages. Being a platform requires you to be trustworthy as a brand. Can customers, especially Millennials, trust you to do what you say you will do and be transparent about what you are already doing? Can they trust you enough to want to share your message and product with their friends? Will they want to align themselves with your brand and what you stand for? All it takes is one social media post to go viral, and the younger generations are best equipped to do this. If they spot an irregularity, you can be pretty sure they will call out your bluff publicly.

Preference #4: Speed & Instant Gratification

'Millennials have come to expect connectivity and instantaneousness in where they live, work and play. Convenience is important for them. Brands need to be timely with information and consistent with messages coming through different spectrums.'

— Barry Lapides, an attorney at law firm Berger Singerman[28]

---

[28] B. Lapides, 'Tips for marketing to generation Y and millennials', *Business News Daily*. (28 April 2023), https://www.businessnewsdaily.com/6602-selling-to-generation-y.html

Millennials are known as the digital natives for a reason. They are used to being bombarded with information every moment of the day. It is nothing new for them and as a result, their brains have evolved to process inputs faster than ever before. According to research, Millennials have a twelve-second attention span whereas Gen Z have an eight-second attention span.[29]

Millennials are on the front end of many important purchases like their first home, first car, work clothes or social expenses for dating or even for marriage. They know they can walk into any retailer, find a product, look through their phone for reviews, and compare while they are still in the store. If convinced that the product is legit, they can choose to buy it immediately from the store or get it ordered online if it is cheaper. There are millions of 'unboxing' videos from toys to gadgets that educate them. Social media has made it even more convenient with options like Facebook shop that allows you to shop while browsing social media. You can be watching Netflix and if you liked what the actress was wearing, you could actually search it up through certain websites to identify the product.

This group of consumers are making gut decisions about what interests them in a matter of nanoseconds. Once they decide something is interesting or worth their time, they click and assess the content for about eight to twelve seconds. According to Sarah Weise, author of *Instabrain*, Gen Z scroll their social media feeds 2.5 times more than Millennials because there is so much noise out on these platforms. That is why Facebook ads have switched to *relative* scroll times. For a specific individual, Facebook can measure how fast they typically scroll, and can detect if a specific ad was noticed based on a noticeable slowing of the scroll. The more people slowed down to view your ad, the more people likely viewed it. When it comes to transactions, this generation does not tolerate sluggishness. They expect speed and efficiency in everything they do. That's why your interface must be lightning fast,

---

[29] Abby Sklencar, 'Social Media Marketing And the Gen Z Attention Span', *Online Optimism.* https://www.onlineoptimism.com/blog/social-media-marketing-and-the-gen-z-attention-span/#:~:text=Whilepercent20Genpercent20Zpercent20isper cent20a,Zper cent20isper cent20aboutper cent208per cent20seconds

with seamless transitions between disparate touchpoints. They should work flawlessly on a mobile. Sloth is a sin for this generation. They live in an era where nearly everything is available immediately and Millennials love this. This accessibility eventually led to Millennials developing shorter attention spans. They don't even need to leave the house to go grocery shopping, watch a movie, get food, or talk to friends and loved ones. The short attention span of the young consumers poses a major challenge for social media platforms and marketers. Platforms like TikTok have quickly risen to popularity due to short-form videos. They are easily digestible and only require a short amount of attention before moving on to the next video. Other platforms have created versions of what TikTok offers to compete with its growing popularity of the short-form video platform. Instagram launched Reels while YouTube launched Shorts.

Social listening is a valuable tool that allows brands to track all mentions of their company or product online. This way, they can ensure they never miss a keyword mention or important customer interaction. Take the time to respond to your audience's comments, reviews, feedback, and direct messages to foster engagement and brand loyalty. This also applies to the customer experience if they are looking to make a purchase. This means that a company's e-commerce site should be mobile-optimized, with an easy user experience to ensure an optimal mobile experience. Optimizing the company website for mobile is critical if companies want to succeed in the millennial market. It is essential to recognize that millennials value their time and expect convenience. They don't like having to wait for long load times or fumble their way through lousy navigation. In fact, they will leave quickly if your site is not mobile-optimized, user-friendly, and easy to navigate.

With more than 60,000,000,000 messages sent out on digital platforms each day, brands have to get creative to stand out. With technology being a constant part of our upbringing, we have become used to always seeing something new. It has become customary to have multiple devices in one household. With multiple devices, this generation has become used to multitasking and jumping between activities at a high rate.

While a shorter attention span among viewers may seem like a negative thing, it has the potential to benefit brands. Many brands have opted to use TikTok and Instagram reels to market to the younger consumer group. TikTok is a platform that provides users with a feed curated to what they interact with the most, also known as the 'For You' page. This gives brands a unique opportunity to market to TikTok users. Additionally, due to the concise video options that TikTok provides, brands can use this to get the most critical information to users in a short period. A shorter TikTok video has a higher chance of keeping the attention of its users than a longer one.

Social media marketing is critical to reaching this demographic. These tools have allowed Millennials to stay in touch not just with each other, but with businesses too. With the internet at their fingertips and the ability to find information quickly, Millennials value immediacy. That's why engaging and responding to your current and potential customers as quickly as possible is essential. To foster brand loyalty amongst Millennial followers, it is important to give them your undivided attention. This means you need to be poised to respond. You gotta be ready to answer direct messages, reply to comments, and treat your followers with respect. Considering that 47 per cent of consumers define a best-in-class brand as one that offers strong customer service, timely responses are an essential part of any brand's social strategy. Millennials would buy from a brand that responds to inquiries more quickly than their competitors. This illustrates the importance of responsiveness in maintaining consumer loyalty and ensuring financial goals are met. In the past, we may have had little to no interaction directly with our consumers. But with emails, private messaging, and commenting, we are able to maintain correspondence with consumers to build rapport and trust. The best part? You can use all this instant feedback from real-life customers to know what they really want and deliver that to them! It's like having a focus group at all times.

Dave Kerpen, author of the book, *Likeable Business* shares a story in his book that illustrates this point. In May 2011, Emerson

College Phonathon had its end-of-the-semester party. They asked their local burrito spot, Boloco, to cater to the event. However, when the supervisors went to pick up their order, they were informed it wasn't ready. Anxious and angry at the situation, the kids tweeted about their situation because they knew that Boloco is known for responding to complaints on Twitter. At the very least, they could get an apology and hope to get a few extra free burritos. Three minutes after they tweeted, the CEO John Pepper apologized for the inconvenience and gave them his cell phone number. When the students hung up the phone, they discovered that their boss was the one who had accidentally submitted the wrong pickup time for the order. They felt awful for their mistake and mortified that they had made such a fuss when Boloco wasn't even in the wrong. However, team Boloco took care of the situation by recognizing its urgency, wrapped up the Burritos in record time and in time for the party. Boloco is known for its commitment to responding efficiently and effectively to each and every customer. On Twitter, this means that no tweet is left unanswered, and every mistake is apologized for and rectified with a free menu item. They are thoroughly appreciative of feedback and respond to it in a genuine way. Sure, negative feedback can sting but John Pepper says that people are hurt when they feel ignored and happy when they realize their voice matters.

Social media amplifies every opinion, which can be a blessing or a curse depending on how great your product or organization is as well as how responsive your customer service teams are. With the conversation moving online, some organizations are moving their customer service teams online as well, allowing for speedy responses. Depending on the size of your business, it might not be possible to respond to every single person. Responding efficiently and effectively requires proper prioritization. The Millennial who has a high follower number on Instagram or a frequent Google reviewer can cause more damage to your business than a competitor can. Many organizations are adopting chatbots on their websites to address customer inquiries and address problems as soon as possible. Building extensive frequently asked questions (FAQs) can help your fans to get the information they need. Building a forum around FAQs can empower your fans to help one another. Look into the processes your company can put into place so that every contact point is responded to promptly. It's not just about online engagement, it's about ensuring no one feels ignored when they attempt to connect with your business. No one likes to be put on hold for thirty-five minutes. It may not seem like it, but you are saying a lot when you say nothing at all. Ignoring a problem doesn't make it go away. Responding is the way to win them over, even if it means saying you're sorry.

Here's an interesting find: When Millennials decide they are interested in a brand or a personality, they go nuts. Once you capture their attention, it is like a switch that has flipped. They turn into mini-stalkers and deep dive into the very thing that sparked their interest. They search for every shred of information they can find and geek out on it. In fact, the harder the information is to find, the greater the gratification. Once they decide they like a brand, they want to know everything. They crave behind-the-scenes stories coupled with personal insights and authentic content. They expect photos, videos, stories, and more to get slice-of-life content. They will use different social media platforms to learn more about the brand or personality. They will watch every YouTube video their favourite creator ever made and find out all the other significant details about them as much as possible. So as brands or creators, it is important to put out all sorts of content that meets these unique needs.

Brands of all sizes across all industries will be tasked with recognizing this new normal and adapting if they want to benefit from the purchasing power of Millennials, which is growing by the day. The verdict is clear: It's much harder to capture the attention of these young consumers. But once you do, they will tune out everything else in order to focus and learn while being excited at the same time. They want to be able to go down the rabbit hole and have a feast on every piece of content that has been put out. That's how influencers attain massive growth. All it takes is one piece of content to get their attention from the masses, and you're off on your own. If you want to really make them work hard, scatter your content across the different social media platforms to get them really involved. Their need for instant gratification will drive them to do a deep dive as long as you have enough content laid out for them.

Preference #5: Humour . . .

[Source: https://www.linkedin.com/posts/the-marketing-millennials_we-got-this-ps-if-havent-checked-out-activity-6987398946620928000-mEzt/?trk=public_profile_like_view]

'I'm a young adult, and I've been bombarded with paid ads for as long as I can remember. The marketing pitches have gotten old, and I find them a real turn-off.' Anushk Mittal , Founder of Memeois[30]

When was the last time you saw an ad so funny that you wanted to share it with all your friends? Bringing humor into marketing can

---

[30] K. Tama-Rutigliano, 'Council post: Memes: A digital marketing tool for every industry', *Forbes*, (10 August 2018). https://www.forbes.com/sites/forbescommunicationscouncil/2018/08/10/memes-a-digital-marketing-tool-for-every-industry/?sh=ef7ba682664a

be a good way for you to help consumers better cope with a polarized and violent world. So let's make marketing fun again. Research by Kantar shows that humour has been declining since 2020, with fewer ads being categorized as 'light hearted' or 'funny'. Oracle did a study that said 90 per cent of people were more likely to remember a brand's ad more if it was funny, while 48 per cent mentioned that they didn't feel they had a relationship with brands if they didn't make them smile or laugh. In an age of impersonal digital media, building social media connectedness through nostalgia is an easy way for companies to leverage the optimistic feelings that often accompany walks down the memory lane. If you had access to the internet in the 1990s, you would probably remember the frustration of your internet connection getting cut because your mom's friend kept calling the house landline. It wasn't a fun experience then, especially when you're in the middle of an important project, but looking back, it is a funny memory. Associating brand messaging with positive references from the 1980s, 1990s and 2000s humanizes brands, forging meaningful connections between the past and the present.

You Need to Be an Insider to Make the Joke

Brands today are afraid of 'cancel culture' and worry that while it may be entertaining, it might not do much for sales. It is critical to get the tone right. Millennials love content that is relatable, because it allows us to feel 'in' on a joke. Aligning marketing strategies with emotions have already been proven to be successful, but tapping into fond memories can be an invaluable tactic, especially for engaging millennials. Coca-Cola, Microsoft, Lego, and even Herbal Essences hair care products are just some brands stepping back in time to reignite campaign strategies of the past. Pokemon GO is an extraordinary example of combining nostalgia with marketing and modern relevance. Reliving positive memories and beloved icons from the past feels good.

Brands have to talk to the Millennials in order to get a grasp over our sense of humour. A copy-and-paste template may not always work for all brands. This means you really have to understand the lens we experience the world with. For instance, if you have used a Nokia phone before, you can probably relate to this meme below:

Millennials also enjoy poking fun at nostalgic experiences we share as a generation, like Microsoft WordArt, which was the go-to software for projects when Millennials were in school.

As a business goes online, it becomes important for them to market its products and services efficiently. Today, social media plays the biggest role in the success of any business. As per the ongoing Nokia has the best mobile battery life trend, social media marketing memes is one of the most popular and demanding forms of marketing strategies that is adopted by many businesses around the world. Meme marketing has become the most favourable and highly beneficial form of marketing amongst brands for one simple reason: Humour.

Nokia has the best mobile battery life

[Source: https://m.facebook.com/Telekomnetworksmalawi/ photos/a.319931251431944/910485875709809/?type=3&p=28]

Nobody can resist a funny image. That's why memes are engaging to all audiences, especially Millennials. Meme (pronounced 'Meem') marketing is a concept where a particular marketer uses a humorous image, video, giphy, or simply a text that relates to the Millennial generation. It can be sarcastic, dark, deep, and can be used to spread information or a joke rapidly using the internet. Memes have a special power: they utilize hidden messages and emotions, many that relate to the young consumers.

[Source: https://www.tiktok.com/@wendys/video/
6938138199961210118?lang=en]

Memes have become the language of Millennials. Its strength lies in its relevance. Being up to date with the latest social media trends is one of the most useful ways that can benefit businesses and keep them ahead of their competitors. A meme that is spot on can spread like wildfire with millions of impressions in a day. An average Millennial looks at twenty-thirty memes a day. Meme sharing is a trend amongst Millennials, be it on WhatsApp or Instagram. When Millennials see an email ad or an SMS promoting a product, Millennials might just delete or ignore the ad. However, when they come across a meme, they know there's a chance for them to get a good laugh out of it. Interestingly, when Millennials come across ads in the form of memes, they engage with it more than a regular ad.

Dollar Shave Club ✔
about 3 months ago

It's 2016. Who says a lady's razor has to be pink? Dollar Shave Club delivers amazing razors (to both genders) for just a few bucks a month.
Try the Club today.

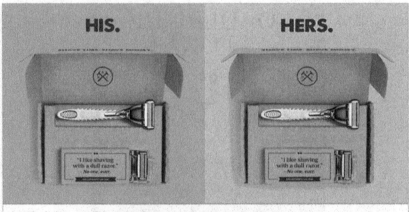

[Source: https://relevantlymarketing.com/news/
dollar-shave-club-ad-sales-through-facebook]

'When I see memes, I may or may not be interested in the [company's] product or service. Either way, I know I'm in for a good laugh! That's often enough to pique my interest and hang around to see what else they have.'

—Anushk Mittal, founder of Memeois

Memes trigger certain emotions which are highly relatable to Millennials. It is the use of positive emotions and humour as a way to break the ice and engage with prospects. Memes are considered to be even more meaningful than emojis because they can convey even more nuanced feelings. Everyone from the president of the United States to Elon Musk is part of meme culture.

When they come across a meme that is relatable, they share it with others who can relate to the same. It is a very cost-effective way for brands to achieve their marketing goals by spending less money on advertising and marketing. Companies using memes for advertising can leave a long lasting impression on the audience. If a particular meme goes viral, it can leave a good impression on potential and existing customers and hence is seen as a good way to build a brand reputation and trust amongst the customers.

One of the best brands to utilize the power of humour is Wendy's. In 2021, they held a #NationalRoastDay, where they roasted and poked fun at anyone or any brand that's in the mood for it on Twitter. The caveat? You've got to ask them to roast you i.e. they won't roast you out of the blue.

[Source: https://www.today.com/food/wendy-s-takes-twitter-national-roast-day-today-t208870]

This got them a lot of international media coverage, generating millions of views, conversations, trending all over social media. All of this without spending a single cent. What can you learn from this? It pays to have a personality on social media. A distinct persona that you want to be known for. If your brand was a real person, what would they act like? Sound like? Talk like? Wendy's personality is that of a friend that occasionally likes to tease you and make fun of you, all in good fun. Products and commercials are not the only way you get in touch with Millennials. You have to engage the young generation in a way that allows you to stay in their heads rent-free. The clearer your personality, the longer you live rent-free in the minds of your consumer.

Think about It

- What do you want your brand to be known for?
- What personality traits stand out for your brand?
- Which of these preferences is your brand already appealing to?
- Have you done surveys or interviews with Millennials to know how they perceive you?
- Which brands do you personally like to be associated with as partners?
- What values would you like to highlight as a brand?
- How can you incorporate these preferences of Millennials into your marketing strategies?

Chapter 4

How to Build a Human Connection in a Digital World

When Covid-19 hit, it disrupted marketing in a very significant way. Now, more than ever before, consumers are making intuitive decisions. All the hype marketing isn't working the way like it did pre-pandemic.

Thanks to the internet today, you can find your audience. You can build a business, create a product, and build wealth and solve people's problems by uniquely expressing yourself through the internet. This rings true for brands as well. We live in an age of infinite leverage. The newest form of leverage, according to investor Naval Ravikant, are digital assets and media. These are what we call products with no marginal cost of replication. It started with the printing press, accelerated with broadcast media, and now it has really blown up with the internet. This book is a form of leverage. Before I became an author, the only way for me to reach a large audience was by speaking at conferences. Having a physical book gives me more leverage, as it can reach a lot more people around the world without requiring my presence. Still, getting my book across to different people across the globe takes time. A digital copy of this book, however, generates incredible leverage for me as it can be easily accessed by people across the globe instantly.

We live in an age of leverage and as a business, you want to be leveraged as much as possible so that you have a huge impact. A leveraged marketer can outproduce a non-leveraged marketer by a factor of thousands. That's why now is the best time for marketers to create the highest form of leverage through media, specifically digital media.

Why Create Digital Media Assets?

Back in the agricultural age, the primary asset was land. In the industrial age, the primary asset was owning a factory or the ability to organize labor under one roof. The primary asset in the digital age are digital assets. We are going through a transition from the industrial age to the digital age and the younger generation in businesses, family businesses particularly, are going to have conflicts with older generations over which assets need to be developed and owned. The older generations naturally lean towards factory, real estate, machinery and plant equipment whereas the younger generation lean towards digital assets. Even physical assets like owning a hotel need to be adorned with digital assets to drive traffic. That's why we look at photos, videos, and all sorts of content before we pick and choose the hotel we want to stay in. I can assure you, photos make a huge difference when it comes to picking a hotel in a foreign country you have never been to before.

Google answers almost every question that comes to mind. Social media connects you with like-minded individuals around the world. E-commerce allows you to sell products to a global marketplace. Information is freely available, people are instantly connected, and markets are globally accessible. Consumers are experiencing brands on multiple platforms. They watch videos on their phones, read blogs, follow people on Twitter, and subscribe to emails. People experience the world through their smartphones and computers as much as the 'real world'. They make buying decisions based on what they see and hear on social media. These changes have already transformed the business landscape and the rate of change is speeding up.

Digital assets have three superpowers. It transcends time, space and wear-and-tear. Whatever video or blog you upload will be available the moment you upload it and in the next five to ten years because it will still be on the internet. It will transcend time. If you record a video with black hair, looking all young and fashionable, trust you will look just as good on the video ten years later even if your hair has turned all white.

As soon as you create a media asset in Singapore, it can be instantly available in Beijing, Bangkok, or Bangalore at no additional cost. It's available all over the world instantaneously. Most interestingly, digital assets don't depreciate. They transcend wear and tear. A thousand people could watch your videos and read your blogs and it will not have worn itself out. You could take a video of the best salesperson in the company, put that online, and that could do more for the company than an army of 200 salespeople. Digital assets have these superpowers that empower a business. It allows a business to open up in new markets across time and space with longevity.

Digital Media Assets Nurture Strong Relationships

Now, at this point, you must be thinking, what is the purpose of creating these digital assets? Yes, they provide leverage, but leverage for what? In an online world, the key differentiator between those who can leverage the internet well and those who struggle to leverage the internet comes down to one simple factor: Relationships.

Millennials expect a two-way, mutual relationship with companies and their brands. It's called the reciprocity principle. Through the feedback Millennials express online and offline, Millennials influence the purchases of other customers and potential customers. They also help define the brand itself. Companies can expect that a positive brand experience will prompt Millennials to take favourable public action on behalf of their brand. A disappointing experience can turn a Millennial into a vocal critic who will spread the negative word and warn their loved ones through social media, reviews and blogs. Sometimes, those criticisms go viral. So as a brand, here's something for you to ponder:

Are you able to build deep relationships with people whom you have never met before and get them to buy your products or services? Is it possible for you to do that while building a relationship with the people you are reaching out to? For ages brands have been relying on advertisements to bring in sales. However, with the internet, it has enabled and empowered brands to build strong relationships with the people they connect with. Whether you are a small business owner, a solopreneur, self-employed or a marketer in an established firm, you have to understand the nuances of building strong relationships online and on social media. That's how influencers have risen to fame. They have leveraged social media platforms to put out content that has in return, helped them build relationships at scale. The people who see value in their content become followers and over time, they do business with the influencers because they have built up trust with them. That's why gaining followers has become quite the craze amongst many business owners, entrepreneurs and self-employed professionals.

A lot of people have social media accounts and a good number of connections. They know what their goals are, where to post and when exactly to post content. And yet, a lot of them struggle to see the return on investment of their time and money of utilizing social media. So, what are they missing?

The answer is connection. Social media was built for human connection and connecting with people is still the best way to convert customers online. All of the automation, scheduling, and analytics tools in the world won't help you if you can't build relationships with your followers and potential customers. The question to ponder about is this:

How can you connect more deeply with people through social media and the online space?

To answer that question, we have to begin with understanding how people build relationships with businesses in general. Think about the last time you met someone new at a networking event and started chatting. You probably started out with some common, general topics. No one goes directly into sharing about their medical history or family drama. Neither do they dive into a sales pitch-fest. Over time, as you stay in touch with that person and gradually become familiar with one another, you start to be more comfortable with the idea of working with them. The beauty of social media is that we have the power to build relationships and grow visibility with a large group of people. Previously, achieving this amount of scale was close to impossible for the solopreneur or the small business owner. Creating content today is a permissionless leverage. You don't require the permission of anybody to create content for your business. This empowers you to reach a larger audience

Dunbar's Number

Dunbar's number is the number of meaningful and stable relationships you can have at any one time. The Dunbar's number is actually a series of concentric circles, each standing for qualitatively different kinds of relationships, as shown in the image below. According to Dunbar, the figure of 150 represents the maximum number of individuals with whom we can have a genuine social relationship.

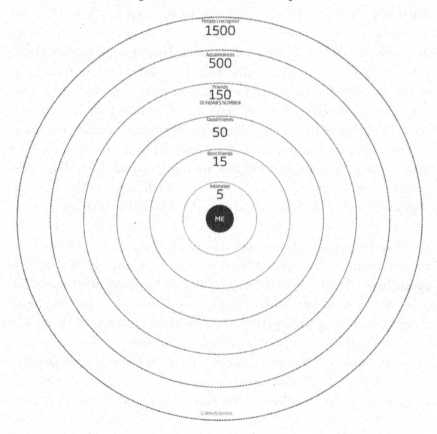

[Source: https://www.newscientist.com/definition/dunbars-number/]

It was invented by psychologist Robin Dunbar, who posits that, in monkeys and apes, there is a correlation between primate brain size and the size of their social groups. In other words, the bigger their brain, the bigger their network. Interesting, huh?

He dug further to see how this applies to humans. According to him, the figure of 150 represents the maximum number of individuals with whom we can have a genuine social relationship. Marketers spend so much time growing their lists, increasing their followers, and marketing to the masses but perhaps there's a better way to look at this. Small, close-knit groups have the power to magnify the epidemic potential of a message or idea. Dunbar lends the idea of focusing on our most established followers instead of looking into expensive marketing methods that bring little to no returns. According to investor Kevin Kelly, to be a successful brand, you don't need millions of followers. You only need a 1000 true fans. To get to these true fans, you have to nurture the first 150 champions. Dunbar's number is the baseline for future success. If you have 150 dedicated and committed followers, ones who have alerts for your brand when you post something online, they will eventually spread the word to others as long as the underlying creative content is proven worth it. A true fan is defined as a fan who will buy anything you produce. They will go to extreme lengths to attend your new launch, buy your books, join your events etc. They share an identity by associating themselves with your product or service. As the number of fans grows, the intensity of the relationship decreases. According to Dunbar, there are a number of concentric circles and each layer is three times the size of the layer preceding it: 5, 15, 50, 150, 500, 1500, etc. Anything more than 150 and people are known to be mere acquaintances. For any business, the goal is to move prospects closer from the acquaintance (500 pax) range to get them interested in making a purchase.

The number 150 is average, but there's a lot of variation ranging from 100 to 250. Historically, the average size of English villages, church parishes, and military units revolved around the number 150. The 150 number marks the cognitive limit on those with whom we can maintain a stable social relationship involving trust and obligation with.[31]

What's interesting about his study is that he found out in order to trust someone, to feel that you know who they are, you like them and are willing to buy something from them, he found that there's a significant amount of time that someone had to spend and interact with in order to know someone. He found that it took about seven hours to make it to the acquaintance sphere within a short space of time like three months. So for a brand to convert someone from a stranger to a fan, it has to put out seven hours of content online to build the relationship with consumers. The beauty of this is that relationships can be built at scale as long as consumers have put out 7 hours of content for them to interact with. All you have to do is serve your consumers online. How do you do that? To put it simply, you have to add value to them by answering their burning questions about their problems. However, in order to create content that converts into sales, you need to first understand about the new buyer's journey i.e. the zero moment of truth.

Zero Moment of Truth

A few months ago, as I was mindlessly scrolling on Instagram, I was served an ad on a note-taking device. The device is called 'Remarkable 2.0'. The stimulus was a video ad, so I watched the video to learn what this device was. It shared the promise of having all my notes in one place, while being able to sync it on my phone. As someone who carries far too many notebooks to capture inspiration in the moment when it strikes, it felt like a good product to get. So what did I do? I clicked the 'learn more' button to read more about what the product does. What features does it have? What do people have to say about it? How long does the battery last? How is this different from having an iPad? What do others have to say about this on YouTube?

---

[31] Robin Dunbar, 'Dunbar's Number', *New Scientist*. https://www.newscientist.com/definition/dunbars-number/

That led me to watch a bunch of reviews on the product and along the way I started watching unboxing videos of the same. Those videos educated me of the pros and cons of the device and allowed me to make a conscious decision instead of an impulse purchase. Why am I telling you this?

It's because that little moment is the moment that's changing the marketing rulebook. It's a new decision-making moment that takes place a hundred million times a day on mobile phones, laptops, and wired devices of all kinds. It is a culmination where marketing, information, and decision making happens concurrently. Google has named this moment of research as the 'Zero Moment of Truth'. Zero moments of truths happen all around us.

- A young woman searching for a flat to rent out by looking through listings on the web
- A new mother looking through her mobile phone on what diapers to buy for her newborn baby based on a multitude of factors
- A student in a cafe scanning through the website looking for a mathematics tutor by reading reviews and success stories of past students
- A couple expecting a new child looking through various chat room discussions to decide which Ob-Gyn to pick
- A conference manager sitting at her desk deciding which speaker to pick for her event by browsing through a series of speaker websites

The 'Zero Moment of Truth' is that specific moment when you grab your smartphone or laptop and start learning about a product or service you're thinking about trying or buying. This is how all consumers of all generations live and learn and make decisions today. They look at the content like ratings and reviews on sites, from friends on social media, at home and on the go, and even through watching videos.

The older generations didn't experience the zero moment of truth until recently. Before that, the way they made decisions about buying anything was made in the store. It followed three simple steps:

Stimulus: Your dad is watching a football game and sees an ad for digital cameras. He thinks, 'Wow, that looks good.'

Shelf: He goes to his favourite electronics store, where he finds a beautiful stand-up display for that same digital camera. The packaging looks great, a young sales guy answers all his doubts and questions, and he makes a decision to buy the camera then and there.

Experience: Dad gets home and the camera records beautiful pictures of his family just as advertised. He is happy with his purchase.

Shoppers have always looked into products and done their research even before the internet. The really determined ones would go to the library to read reviews on magazines of the digital cameras they wanted to get a hold on. Others would read consumer reports on different products based on industry journals that has detailed research. Till today, we see many guidebooks for hotels and restaurants which include information that would be useful for the end user. The reason many from the previous generations didn't spend as much time in the zero moment of truth back then was due to lack of easy access. Fresh and detailed information about a given product was not easily accessible back then. The exception has become the rule today.

Procter & Gamble called that moment in the store the 'First Moment of Truth'. According to A.G. Lafley, ex-CEO of P&G,

> 'The best brands consistently win two moments of truth. The first moment of truth occurs at the store shelf, when a consumer decides whether to buy one brand or another. The second one occurs at home, when she uses the brand, and is delighted, or isn't.'

He mentioned this back in 2005 and now there is a critical moment of decision that happens before consumers get to the first moment. Whether you sell phones or watches or handbags, your customer's first impression and possibly their final decision is made during the zero moment of truth. The buying decision journey has changed with ZMOT as a vital new addition to the classic three-step process of stimulus, shelf and experience. Consumers today find and share their own information about products, in their own way, on their own time. Word of mouth is stronger than ever in the digitally archived medium. Our mobile devices are moment of truth machines. As mobile usage grows, zero, first and second moments of truth are converging. Pre-shopping before buying has become a huge part of customer behaviour. In the past, it was confined to big-ticket items such as cars, homes or expensive electronics. Now, people engage in discovery before shopping on very small things. It has crossed all categories of shopping behaviour and has become the norm; it's just the way people buy today. So if dad sees a similar ad for a digital camera while watching YouTube, he googles digital camera reviews and reads comments of the product before he decides to make the purchase. He looks through the variety of content and makes a decision before he even makes it to the store.

Here's what makes the Zero Moment of Truth unique. It happens online, and typically starts with a search on Google, YouTube, Facebook or Instagram. It happens in real time at any time of the day and consumers are in charge. They pull the information they need when they specifically need it as opposed to having it pushed to them by others. Zero Moments of Truth are usually emotional, where the consumer wants to satisfy an emotional craving in finding the best solution.

7-11-4

Marketers who are able to be visible with digital media assets during the Zero Moment of Truth are at an advantage. According to Google, a buyer will spend 7 hours on average in four different locations across eleven touch points before they are ready to make the all-important decision to buy. The four locations could very well be your website, social media pages, on review sites or a live interaction in a shopping mall. A total of eleven touch points are required before they are ready to make the purchase. Your customers will find you at the very moment they are thinking of buying as well as the moment they are going through the research phase—the pre-sell phase of buying. Interestingly, this ZMOT becomes even more important when money is tight for the consumer. So here's the kicker:

- Do you have a plan to win the Zero Moment of Truth when people are searching for your product or service?
- Do you have enough media assets online to guide consumers who are lost and afflicted?
- When you start typing your product or service name, before you finish typing, what search terms fill in automatically below?
- Does your website or your message appear on the top third of the first page results for those searches?
- How does your brand appear in terms of rating through review sites for your category?

The beauty of creating content is that it allows you to scale and duplicate yourself. As mentioned at the start of this chapter, content once produced is able to work on your behalf on building relationships at scale. Individuals from all over the world can consume that content and learn more about who you are as a brand and what you stand for. Of course, you can't just put out anything and everything and expect people to fall in love with your brand. Cat videos get lots of views, likes and shares but I can assure you it won't do anything for your brand if you put it out (unless you sell something related to cats). There has to be a proper strategy around it, which I will cover in depth in Chapter 8.

Before we dive deep into the strategy, it is important that you have a high level of awareness of what you are capable of as a marketer. There are five key ways to creating content. You can create content in the form of videos, where people get to watch and listen to you. There is auditory content in which the audience can listen to the content that is put out. Next, there is content you can write so that others can read about it and lastly, you can run events where participants can be engaged with a multi-sensory approach. With new paradigms like the Metaverse becoming a thing, I won't be surprised to see people have networking sessions using these powerful technologies. Lastly, if you have an eye for design, then that in itself can be considered a specific format to dive deeper into. Some people are just naturally better at designing, but they disregard the skill because they see it only as a hobby and didn't learn it 'professionally'. Ignore the naysayers. If you're good at something, hold on to it because it is your unfair advantage. In short, the five different ways in which you can create content are:

- Watch
- Listen
- Read
- Do
- Design

In the same way you enjoy consuming content in a particular format, you will also most likely be comfortable in creating content in a particular format. The key is in finding out which method is the best for you to embark on. Some people are really good at writing, whereas others can speak for hours without stopping (but don't quite like showcasing themselves on video) and there are some who seem like a natural on camera. All formats work, but especially when you are starting out, it is vital to pick the one that comes to you almost effortlessly and double down on that method to generate content. Take five minutes to figure out which strengths you already have and which resources are readily available to you.

I say this because I've seen so many small business owners, solopreneurs and self-employed professionals struggle to create content. Sometimes they pick the format that seems to be the trend (vertical videos for TikTok!) when they're much more comfortable and competent in writing thoughtful articles. Start with your current skills and available time and you will make a lot more progress than attempting to jump on a bandwagon that requires you to spend more time in picking up more skills. If you are aiming to maintain a certain level of quality in your content, you have to realize there is a trade-off when you attempt the new ways of content creation that are outside your comfort zone. Whenever you are attempting to do something new, you have to go through the 'J-curve', which basically looks like this:

Your performance will take a dip when you start out because you have not put in the hours to become competent in it. If writing doesn't come easily to you, the time you invest in getting good at writing will slow you down considerably. If you are much more comfortable with recording videos, start with that. Going after the shiny new object (in this case, vertical video format of creating content) can end up being a huge drain on your time and energy. Yet, I see people do it all the time. I don't blame them. A lot of gurus advocate the best, fastest, and easiest way to get more done as a marketer that people simply listen without thinking about how it applies to them. Unless you're looking to be busy, following this method won't make you any more productive. I will go through in detail the pros and cons of different content types and how you can maximize the content you create through various methods in Chapter 8. If you are still not clear about which format to create to content in, I've got a simple decision matrix to help you out.

The ICE framework forces you to ask three questions about your marketing strategy before you take the time to implement it. On a scale of 1 to 10, with one being the lowest and ten being the highest, score yourself on the conditions below.

1. Impact: How impactful could this format be for my marketing?
2. Confidence: How confident am I that this strategy would draw in potential customers?
3. Ease: Given my skills and resources, how easy would it be to create content in this format?

You score each question above from 1 to 10 (with ten being the highest, one being the lowest), total the scores, and the highest score will be the best format for you to create content in.

Format	Video	Audio	Write	Events
Impact				
Confidence				
Ease				
Total				

By the way, this decision matrix works for many tricky situations where you don't know which option to pick. Let's say I want to lose some weight, but I don't know which way to choose, this matrix helps.

Option 1: Swimming Ten Laps Daily

Impact: Swimming is one of the best ways to get lean. If done consistently, I am pretty confident of losing the extra fat and gaining more muscle. I will give it a 8/10 score for impact.

Confidence: I am a novice at swimming. I can swim, but I know there is a lot of improvement to be made for me to be able to swim ten laps without stopping. My confidence level in my technique is not high, so I will give it a 4/10.

Ease: My swimming complex is close to my home, so getting there isn't a hassle. The only issue is if it rains, it might affect my swimming habit and it has been raining quite a bit lately. I'll give it a 6/10.

Total Score: 18/30

Option 2: Running 2 km Daily

Impact: I have lost a lot of weight considerably fast by running. I know this because I've done this before and it has even worked for me. I'll give this a 9/10 for impact.

Confidence: During my army days, I have run long distances not because I liked it, but because I had no choice. Therefore, I know I can do this and it can help me lose weight for sure. My confidence in running is 9/10.

Ease: I have always enjoyed running in the park, which is nearby. There are lots of sights and sounds, and I find that therapeutic. I also can listen to podcasts while running which makes me even more productive so I like that. So I guess I can give this category a 10/10 for ease.

Total score: 28/30

Now, based on the scores, it is pretty easy for me to make a decision. I can add more options to illustrate the point but I'm sure you got the gist. Use this exact technique to identify which format you should focus on creating content and use that as you unfair advantage. Many people don't lean in to what comes almost naturally to them and make their lives difficult by attempting things that require them to pick up new skills and competencies. This is usually a huge time sink and an even bigger demoralizing factor.

As the world gets more complicated with technology, it becomes even more important for us marketers to have clarity over our strengths and weaknesses. Sure, there will always be the next shiny object that will attract our attention. However, if we want to skip the J-curve and hit the ground running, the best way to start is by leveraging what you are already good at, based on the total score you get from the ICE matrix.

Now that you know what's the best method for you to build relationships at scale, let's dive deeper into learning more about your audience, the Millennial consumer and their behavioural psychology in the next chapter!

Think about It

- Do you have a good number of digital assets for your business?
- Are you sweating your business assets i.e. are they working well to generate results for you?
- Have you adopted the Zero Moment of Truth principle for your business?
- Do you have a nurturing sequence online to grow your relationships with your prospects?
- Have you identified which formats you can generate content in using the ICE matrix?
- How much content do you currently have that allows you to build a relationship with your ideal clients?

Chapter 5

Audience: Building Trust at Scale with Behavioural Psychology

Most entrepreneurs mistakenly think that their company is all about them, but it's not. On the contrary, your business should be all about your customer. If you want customers to come and find you to provide solutions to their problems, you must know your customer at a deeper level. The first step is in becoming obsessed with your dream customer. Companies that are obsessed with their own products will inevitably fail. When I say obsessed, I mean getting a PhD in understanding your customers. It is about understanding their mindset, their behaviours and everything else about them, almost to a fault. In many cases, entrepreneurs who start out on their own do so because they faced a problem that had no better solutions which prompted them to find a solution to it themselves. They end up figuring out the solution to the problem they faced.

Our mess becomes our message.

I remember being very fascinated about coaching other Millennials because I went through a difficult period of time during my teenage years.

Sometimes, even the people closest to you don't know what's best for you. Which is dangerous when you don't know what you want. Back when I had just finished my O levels, I was faced with a decision to pick the science or arts or commerce stream for my A levels. At that age, I had no idea what would suit me the best so I asked around. When I asked my Dad, he said, 'Son, you should choose commerce because it's in your blood.' My dad's an accountant.

When I asked my friends, they said, 'You're Indian! Of course you must choose IT/computing, la.'

Plus the IT industry was talked about as the most lucrative thing to pursue back then.

The career prospects (read salary) were promising. So that's what I did. I took up the science stream which included a computing subject C++. Worst. Decision. Ever. I ended up realizing that computer languages and I don't get along very well. While I could string sentences together in English effortlessly, I could barely grasp what a string was in C++ language. And I failed my A levels with flying colours. Looking back, it's clear to me I should have picked the arts stream. But I didn't have the self-awareness of my strengths back then. Which is why I'm passionate to coach youths who make career decisions based on such headlines that come out in the newspapers:

Fresh tech graduates from S'pore universities bag highest starting pay of $5,600: survey.

It's a surefire way to find yourself in a quarter life crisis. I'm lucky I only had to suffer two years for my lack of self-awareness. Many youths still base their career decisions by jumping on bandwagons or following their friends (or their crush). Eventually, they find themselves in a place of self-doubt and low self-esteem, despite ticking all the boxes they were told to, by their parents, teachers and mentors. Are Millennials at fault? I don't think so. On the contrary, I think the systems we have in place are outdated. And that needs to change.

Today, my career in speaking about Millennials happened because of the mess I found myself in. I push out the message on how Millennials have grown up differently and why the organizations and systems around us must be agile and adapt to bring out the best from this generation.

When you become frustrated about a problem that you are having, you look for a solution and when you cannot find a solution that gives you the results you desire, you embark on a journey to find your own solution. That problem paves the way for your business and your mess becomes your message.

In order to do that, you need to find your customers, persuade them to follow you, and hopefully change their lives with the products and services you sell. Instead of focusing on the next ad campaign, focus on entering the conversation that is already taking place in your customer's mind. All humans either move away from pain or towards pleasure.

Moving away from pain:

- I'm overweight and don't fit into my clothes like I used to
- I hate working at my job
- I feel awkward when I am at social gatherings and I don't know how to carry a conversation with them

Moving towards pleasure:

- I want to get eight-pack abs
- I want to start my own company and have freedom over my time
- I want to be charismatic and charming when it matters the most—during social gatherings or stakeholder meetings

Consumer Awareness

The millennial consumer has no lack of choice. Brands eager to meet their needs provide everything from personalized services to extensive product lines and reams of information. They are inundated with options, opinions and information to a point that they may feel unsure about their purchase decisions, including who to trust and what to believe. So it is up to brands, in this age of information, help Millennial consumers navigate the complex, emotional process of making purchase decisions. According to a Kantar/Quantum report in 2021, 81 per cent of people who have difficulties making purchase decisions say it's too much because they have too many options or too much information.[32]

---

[32] https://www.thinkwithgoogle.com/intl/en-apac/consumer-insights/consumer-journey/decode-consumer-buying-behaviour-purchase-decisions/

For brands to help Millennials make purchase decisions with confidence, it pays to first understand how the consumer decision-making process has evolved. Throughout our history, problems were caused by an information deficit. They were puzzles you solved by finding new data. However, we are no longer living in an information-scarce world. In fact, we are living in the exact opposite. We now have a big mound of data in front of us and the job as a consumer is to sift through the data, make sense of the data, prioritize it, trash everything that isn't important, and zone in on what is really important.

According to Malcom Gladwell, 'The ability to look at a series of data points and appropriately rank them is one of the hardest and most valuable things we can do to assist people in making sense of complicated decisions . . .'

To make things easier for consumers, brands need to be available both mentally and physically. What I mean by this is that brands have to be able to be 'top-of-mind' and highly recognizable to consumers to be 'mentally available'. Physical availability refers to the process of being able to make the purchase—which should be seamless and easy—whether it is through having one's products stocked in the store or making the online shopping process simple and straightforward.

First and foremost, marketers need to understand the mental journey of a consumer before they even make a purchase. It is critical to go deeper into their behavioural psychology in order for us to market effectively to them. Yes, that means you have to understand what is going through the Millennial consumer's mind as they are contemplating making a purchase. As the legendary direct marketing copywriter, Robert Collier, said,

'You must always enter the conversation already taking place in the customer's mind.'

You need to know the conversation that they're having in their head about your product or service, and you need to know that conversation inside and out. Many marketers think they know who their customers are, but far too often, they really don't. Sometimes, it's because they take shots in the dark, or don't do any research at all. Otherwise, it's because they do the wrong kind of research and fall victim to identifying their clients based purely on demographics data only. Most marketers focus on what they know about their customers and their problems but they never ask themselves, 'What do consumers know about me and my products?'

This is a big problem. When you ask this question, you will find it easier to curate the content you need to create and come up with a targeted marketing plan. It also helps you with the copy to draw the consumer in, whether they visit your website, your social media profiles or your landing pages. When you understand what your prospects already know about you, your product, or service, and the problem they have with it, it will be much easier to convert them into buyers. This allows you to immediately grab their attention and draw them into your message. For example, let's assume you're selling a product on the importance of setting up landing pages. If you are selling to a group of people who know what landing pages already are, the way you draw their attention is by saying something like,

Thirty-four landing pages that helped us double our sales.

But if you're selling to a family business owner who has no idea what a landing page is, that sentence would fall flat because they don't understand the product. That's why for those people who have low awareness of the product, you can use a different sentence like:

How I doubled my sales by using this one piece of software?

Do you see the difference? Do you see how the consumer's awareness level of your product is critical in determining the copy you write in your content? That's why it's important to ask yourself,

What do consumers know about me and my products?

The point here is this. When your consumers already know, like, and trust your product, selling is a lot easier. All you have to do is present your product and make an offer. Now you have to ask yourself if this is true for your product? Chances are your potential clientele are not constantly thinking about your product or service and chances are you don't have the brand equity that big companies like Apple and Nike have. The best way to grow your customer's awareness of your products and services is by understanding the concept of tapped and untapped markets.

The Untapped Market

One of the best ways to grow market share in the market is to start with appealing to a market that largely remains untapped. But before I share about the untapped market, you need to first understand what the tapped market looks like. Let's start with the top of the pyramid. In any given market, 3 per cent of people are ready to buy. This is the tapped market. Look at any ad you see and you will realize that the Facebook ad, YouTube ad, or newspaper/TV/radio ad are all appealing to the individual who realizes they have a problem and are looking in the market for the best solution for them. They are ready to swipe their credit card once they find a solution for their problem. A lot of the ads we see today are reaching out to this group that is out in the market looking for a ready solution. Even your repeat buyers and most loyal fans fall into this category. Selling to this group of people is relatively easy if they have a genuine need. A high percentage of the 3 per cent will buy. A mother that headed out of the house (without any diapers in her bag) is ready to buy diapers when she realizes her infant just soiled her diapers. She has an urgent need and she knows what brand she wants to purchase.

Even consumers in this stage, who are aware of your products and services, need a little bit of convincing. They might know the name of your product and some of the benefits you claim, but they might need a little bit of nudging to make up their mind. So you still have to show that out of all the similar products or services out there, why yours is the best for them to win them over. It's best to grab this group's attention with the product itself. The problem is, a lot of your competitors are charging towards this 3 per cent of consumers. I call the 3 per cent the 'informed consumer'. Everyone is fighting for the attention of the informed consumer. Competition is fierce in this space where the informed consumer usually is spoilt for choice.

In the movie *Jerry Maguire*, Tom Cruise's character makes an impassioned speech to the girl he loves, trying to convince her how much he cares for her. She finally tells him, 'You had me at hello'. These are your most aware prospects. They know your product and that it can potentially help them get what they want. They might be considering other similar products. The informed consumer has the intent to buy and is at the advanced stages of researching their options to make the purchase. They pretty much know which brand they are leaning towards in terms of purchase. That's why they are called the informed consumer and they make 3 per cent of the entire market. The informed consumers are not only aware of the problem, but they're likely already aware of different solutions too. They're just trying to find the best one. If they see something that meets their needs and wants, they can just put it on their credit card and within minutes, have it added to their cart and send it whizzing from the shop to their door. Unfortunately, not everyone is at this stage.

The untapped market begins at an earlier stage, even before the consumer feels the urgent need to make a purchase to solve his existing problems. This is where they may be in the initial stages of experiencing the pain. For example, an accountant who has been experiencing some light back pain for the past two days is not yet ready to go to a chiropractor. That is because the pain isn't as severe yet. However, if a chiropractor is able to get his attention at this stage, where the pain is in its initial stages, the chiropractor has a chance of building a relationship with this accountant through content. This is what I mean by tapping on the untapped market.

How to Get Consumers to Say 'Shut Up and Take My Money!'

The untapped market is where 97 per cent (60+37) of the whole market is. They consist of two groups. The 'afflicted consumer' and the 'oblivious consumer'. To reach the 97 per cent who aren't ready to buy but might very soon, you have to educate them. When a prospect isn't very knowledgeable on a subject, they are in a state of uncertainty and people choose to 'learn more' before they commit to a purchase. The more informed they are, the higher their chances of buying. Here's the kicker:

If you're the one educating them, you're also the one making sure that when they become an informed consumer, they are buying from you. To ensure this, you must have content that is powerful, insightful, education-based, and not just a promotional ad about your product or service. You have to nurture the relationship over a minimum of seven hours of content, eleven touch points over four different locations. The more you do this, the more you realize that you're changing the dynamics and psychology of the relationship between your business and your potential clientele. You start to notice them putting up their hands to speak to you instead of you having to chase for clients.

The Afflicted Consumer

The afflicted consumers are your somewhat aware prospects. They don't know your product yet, but they're painfully aware of the problem they're facing and they know for sure that they want to do something about it. For consumers at this stage, you need to put in more effort to win them over. The reason being they do not know anything about your product, so they are not ready to compare options. All they care about is solving the problem they have and the outcome they desire. With these types of consumers, you can't craft your content with your product first. They aren't ready to hear about your offers. To build a stronger relationship with them, you need to reflect their pain back to them. They must feel understood and from there on, show that there are solutions to that pain. Out of the different solutions, introduce your solution as one possible option and prove that your product is the best answer for them. Take Abel for instance.

Abel is a forty-year-old man who has been overweight his whole life. When he turned forty, he made a decision to lose weight once and for all. He wanted to look good and ripped, and he knew slimming down will help in achieving that outcome. Since Abel is an afflicted consumer, more work needs to go into getting him to buy. You have to educate him about exercise routines, diet plans, and strength training programs. You also have to let him know why doing one without the other is a plan that is destined to fail.

Consumers like Abel feel lost and go to Google for help. They type in search terms like 'how to lose weight fast' and get Google to sift out the best few sites with the best content. They are looking for direction because they don't know what's best, what's bad, and what's gimmicky from the brands that are putting out marketing content to win his money. So Abel has to find someone who answers his questions, gives him some quick wins and wins over his trust as a brand. Instead, you must start out with the promise of the outcome they desire. Then you show them how your product or service can get them the result they want.

The Oblivious Consumer

The oblivious consumers are your least aware prospects. They don't know about your product or service. They don't know much about you. They sense they have a problem, but they may not be aware of what they really want. They tend to experience psychological tension that sits deep beneath the surface. They bury it and don't do anything about it, distracting themselves with other things going on in their lives. This is known as a dormant tension where the desire or frustration is not being acted upon. There can be a number of reasons people don't act upon it. Sometimes they tried something but it didn't work. Or it isn't considered a painful or urgent matter that needs to be addressed immediately for them. They don't have huge stakes involved. Or it's just not worth the time or money to give it any attention. Sometimes it could be a limiting belief that they're holding on to that is affecting them.

Imagine Matthew has back pain. He's had it for a long time and thought it was there because he was overweight. He associated his back pain with his weight and concluded that nothing could be done about his back pain until he loses weight. What Matthew doesn't know is that chiropractors can solve his back pain issue if they knew he had made the wrong conclusions in his head. Because Matthew has parked the problem as something that cannot be solved; he is oblivious about other solutions to solve the problem. He has a dormant tension sitting beneath the surface waiting to bubble up. When the pain becomes excruciating for him to a point it affects his productivity and work, he transitions into an active buyer in the afflicted consumer stage.

For every person who is actively looking for a product or service, there are hundreds of others who might be interested but are not looking because of some misconceptions they have in their minds. If you went to a soccer match and asked the whole stadium, 'Who here is currently searching for a new car?' few people may raise their hands. But if you asked them 'Who here isn't completely 100 per cent satisfied with the car they have?' many more hands will go up. There is great power in being able to identify a dormant tension people have hidden away in the back of their mind.

How to Get People to Buy Products They Don't Think They Need

In the 1920s, there was a famous marketer by the name of Claude Hopkins. He is seen as one of the great advertising pioneers and father of modern-day marketing. He's famous for creating some of the brands that still exist today like Quaker Oats and Goodyear Tire. One of his success stories include his ability to get a group of oblivious consumers to buy a product they didn't know they needed. In the 1920s, Pepsodent approached Hopkins for help to sell more toothpaste. Back then, only 5 per cent of people brushed their teeth on a daily basis (Yuck! I know). It sounds pretty gross now but back then, our current health standards didn't exist. People used to brush their teeth merely once or twice a week and were probably comfortable walking around with bad breath. Hopkins realized that the best way to increase the sales of Pepsodent toothpaste was to go after the 95 per cent who rarely brushed their teeth. He came up with a brilliant advertising campaign that explained that using toothpaste to remove film from teeth would make people look cleaner and better-looking.

He leveraged good looking people and made it seem like they looked good because they brushed their teeth which made their teeth super white. The tagline was 'Pepsodent Makes Teeth Far Brighter'. He then launched a magazine ad campaign that read,

'Film, a dangerous coating that robs teeth of their whiteness. Here's a way to remove it that quickly restores brilliance'. The copy also mentioned that you had to brush your teeth with Pepsodent every single day, twice, in order to keep your teeth white and clean. It was the cheapest and fastest way to look like a star. By 1957, Pepsodent was so popular it even came up with a jingle, 'You wonder where the yellow went, when you brush with Pepsodent'. Pepsodent suppliers couldn't keep up with the demand and it turned out to be one of the best-selling products of the decade. Those who brushed their teeth went from 5 per cent to 65 per cent within ten years.[33]

The smartest entrepreneurs and marketers sell to those who have dormant needs. They go looking for the underlying psychological tension that hasn't yet fully formed and then they warm people up. The whole idea of learning about the three stages of consumer awareness is to help you realize that you can achieve so much more by creating content that appeals to the oblivious consumer and slowly educate them so that they know more about the process of solving their problem, and they're empowered to make a better buying decision. When you actively and skilfully move people up the awareness journey, where you move the 97 per cent of consumers who are not ready to buy or not even thinking about the problem to becoming your customer right away. Nurture them early on in the process with quality content and you will find it much easier to grow your business.

When it comes to nurturing your consumers and getting them to warm up to your brand, quality content is important. You have to add value to the consumer before they even enter the buying stage. In order to create quality content, all you need is to personalize the content you create to speak directly to the Millennial consumers you are targeting. Amid the flood of information we all have access to, people make snap judgements about whether something is relevant to them or not. As soon as they suspect that something isn't intended directly for them, their interest plummets.

What People Already Want to Buy

If you can connect your product or service to what people already want to buy, your marketing efforts will work wonders for you. People want to buy things they already have a desire for. There are six universal desires that appeal to the mass public. Here's an example.

---

[33] B. Kane, B, *Hook point: How to stand out in a 3-Second world*. (Independently publisher by the author, 2022).

Imagine Dave is a coder who decided to offer his services to small business owners. He proceeds to approach them and tells them that he can go through their website and streamline their website's code for them. He would find the things that made the code bloated and make it much more concise. Basically he offers to take 100 lines of code and turn it into ten lines of code. What are the chances of him being able to sell himself if he markets his services like this? Who wakes up and thinks I wish my website's code was shorter than it is now? This might be nice to have but chances are, no one would probably pay for that. Because it doesn't really matter to the small business owner.

What if Dave switched up his approach and said instead, 'Do you want to make more sales?' He then goes on to explain that fast loading websites can increase their sales significantly and most people have slow loading websites because their website code is bloated. He then proceeds to ask the small business owners if they would like him to audit their website's code to check if it is bloated. What do you think the small business owners would do?

Doesn't it seem a lot more appealing to them? Who doesn't want to make more sales? What's ironic and funny about this is Dave is offering the same exact thing in both scenarios. In the latter example, Dave started his pitch by leading with what small business owners already wanted—more sales! He basically showed what he sold could help them get what they already wanted. No matter what you sell, if you follow this approach and take the time to explain how what you sell helps people get what they want, they will buy what you sell and pay you handsomely for it. You see, it might be obvious to you how your product or service can help people make money, live healthily or get a sense of achievement. But that doesn't mean your consumers have that same level of clarity. You have to break it down and connect the dots for them. But first, let's look at the six different universal desires that appeal to everyone.

1. Financial Well-being

Financial well-being is important to all individuals of all ages. Who doesn't want financial well-being? Of course this doesn't mean everyone wants to be filthy rich. Yet, everyone wants to be certain that they can live their life without the stress of worrying about money. There is a particular appeal for Millennials because they have a debt burden starting from their student debt to their mortgage depending on the stage of life they are at. Some are concerned about their ability to retire, or are struggling to support their children and their parents at the same time. This generation also places a high value on experiences and lifestyle goals, such as travelling and owning a home. We are also seeing a greater number of freelancers and entrepreneurs in this generation working in the gig economy. They want to change their career so that they can earn on their own terms. Sometimes, they just want to manage their money better. In all cases, the driving desire is financial well-being. Most people are interested in this.

2. Healthy Life

Nobody wants to die young. Different people have different levels of health but no one wakes up and thinks, 'I want to be unhealthy'. Sometimes they want to be in tip-top shape, other times they just want to be a little healthier than they already are by trying a new diet or going to the gym. Just like financial well-being, everyone wants to be healthy. As the saying goes:

'The healthy person wants many things. A sick person only wants one.'
—Confucius

With rising healthcare costs, Millennials are facing the highest healthcare costs of any generation, making health a top priority. They are also known to focus more on overall wellness, including physical, mental and emotional health. They value self-care and prioritize activities that promote their overall well-being. 'The Great Resignation' and 'Quiet Quitting' are common workplace terms that are becoming popular via social media platforms because of their focus on health over work. It is also notable that Millennials focus more on prevention over cure. This includes going for regular screenings, check-ups and vaccinations to avoid developing chronic health conditions.

3. Companionship

With social media and digital communication becoming the default form of talking to one another, Millennials are more connected and yet even more isolated than previous generations. This makes social interactions and companionships all the more important for this group. This can be either through family or personal relationships. Because well, nobody wants to be alone. Some people may want to start and raise a family. Others just want someone they can share their life with so that they don't go through old-age alone. There are different aspects of companionship that appeal to different people. The key is to understand that this is a universal desire in all people. It's hard to face the world alone with no one to call family or friends. Many in this generation are delaying marriage and family formation, which is leading to loneliness and a stronger desire for companionship. They are also huge advocates for diversity as they are known to be more accepting of LGBTQIA groups and speak out for diversity at the workplace. 'Love is Love' 'is their mantra and they are attracted to brands that embrace the same.

4. Being Desired

This one applies in multiple ways. Sometimes in a romantic sense, other times in a career sense. Usually the desire tends to lean towards vanity. People always want to feel like they have something that is desirable to others. While this might seem shallow, it is innate in most human beings. The fashion, cosmetics, and dating industry thrives on individuals feeling desired. Being desired holds a particular appeal for Millennials as it provides them with validation. It is a boost for their self-esteem and having received that from their helicopter parents and friendly-adult figures while growing up, they are bound to respond better to brands that help them feel desired. Also, Millennials are mostly in their 20's and 30's which leaves them in the stage of life where they are looking to settle down. Being desired or desirable is also something that will connect well with this group. Sometimes it is also tied in with social status. Being desired can be seen as a marker of success and desirability which elevates social status. It's not surprising to see people clamouring for more followers purely because of this intrinsic need.

5. Supporting a cause

It doesn't have to be something that matters to the entire world, it can be something that matters to the individual. Millennials are very focused on this and love to be able to contribute back to society in some form or the other. They prefer purchasing from brands that do good. It makes them feel like they are contributing to a good cause by paying a little extra on their end. If you can attach your product or service to support a cause that matters to your target audience, you can stand to benefit from it greatly. Millennials are passionate about social issues like climate change, social justice, and equality. They want to use their resources to make a difference and gravitate towards brands that think the same. It is also a form of personal fulfillment for them when they contribute to a cause that is bigger than themselves.

6. Sense of Achievement

What's funny is this achievement can be almost anything. It could be a life goal or something as simple as collecting Pokemon—where we saw people go crazy trying to 'catch em' all'. Even the certificates of attendance you get from going to workshops provide this sense of achievement. Achievement makes people feel good about themselves and if you can offer it, they will pay for it. No matter what product or service you are selling, if you can connect one of these universal desires to what you sell, it will greatly aid in your marketing efforts. Millennials are often described as being ambitious with a high interest in entrepreneurship and desire for growth. The sense of achievement comes from scaling new heights which when shared on social media, gives them a dopamine hit.

In my training workshops, I teach participants to identify their consumer's universal desire. Besides, it doesn't have to be only one universal desire. It can be a combination of them as well. Creating powerful combinations increase the desirability of your product or service.

There you go! You've picked up the pieces to help you map out your own marketing strategy based on your target clientele. Learning about their awareness levels will help you plan out the content you need to create because a consumer has different questions going through their minds at different awareness levels. In the next chapter, we will incorporate the concepts covered in this chapter to understand more about creating content that become digital assets and drive customers to queue up at your doorstep.

Think about It

- Are you able to build trust at scale using digital marketing or social media?
- What are some of the characteristics of Millennials you can bank on to market your products and services?
- What are some of the universal desires your products and services are addressing?
- Which stage are your current consumers at and at which stage do you want to capture their attention?
- How can you map out a strategy using the universal desires, Millennial characteristics and consumer awareness levels to grow your business?

Chapter 6

Assets: Secrets to Creating Content that Generates Demand

'You only need one piece of content to change your life.'
—Gary Vaynerchuck, CEO of VaynerX

Remember Zoe from the Charles & Keith saga that I mentioned in the earlier chapters? It's true. One great piece of content has the potential to change your life. The evidence is all around us. We see so many individuals rise up to fame because of the power of the content they put out on the platforms that allow virality to happen. The million dollar question is, 'What will that one piece of life-changing content be?'

Today, there is a huge segment of influencers who are earning way more than what most senior executives took decades to earn because of the content they put out and the followers they amassed. As a result, we have many young people aspiring to become an influencer themselves. It is now possible for a fifteen year old boy to be sitting in his bedroom and start a group of Telegram for free. He can have thousands of followers and fans worldwide for free. He can talk to all of them across the globe for free. He can write to them for free. He can get them excited about his ideas for free and build a business around it. He can create an e-commerce website easily that is inexpensive.

He can design a brand easily with Canva. He can take payments easily and cheaply. He can send his products whizzing around the world easily and cheaply, all from his bedroom. These are the times we are living in. The reason they are able to do all of this is because they aren't stuck to the idea of marketing their business in a traditional manner. They believe in the power of content. Most people think that these Millennial entrepreneurs are succeeding because they are good with technology, but that is not the reason. While it is true that we live in a new and exciting time, thanks to technology, you need more than tech-prowess to make content work for your business.

Back in 1876 when the first microphone was invented, it fascinated a lot of people. It allowed people to reach a bigger audience because it amplified the human voice. Can you imagine seminars and workshops being sold around the topic of 'How to become a Millionaire with a Microphone' or 'The secrets to Millions by using the Microphone'. Sounds ridiculous, doesn't it? To some people, it seems like the technology i.e. microphone is the reason for the success, but they have completely missed the point. The money doesn't go to the person who knows how a microphone works. It goes to the individuals who know how to sing. So in other words, a bad singer becomes a louder bad singer with a microphone in their hand.

Technology is only useful in the hands of someone who has quality content. Today, the 'microphone' we all have at our disposal is the social media platform. It has the ability to take a message and get it out into the world instantly. Many have become obsessed about leveraging social media as the hot new technology but it is not the platform that makes it popular. It is the content that they create. Social media just makes people louder. Boring content will get ignored on any platform because it is, well, boring. So the message I'm driving at is this: Instead of overly worrying about which platform to focus on, I would advise you to get good at creating content that is engaging, entertaining and most importantly, valuable to the consumer.

How to Create High-quality Content?

We all want to create high quality content, but very few people want to go through the 'pain period' of receiving feedback to make your content improve in quality. Truth is, if you are starting out in content creation, you are going to suck, at first.

A ceramics teacher announced on the opening day that he was dividing the class into two groups. All those on the left side of the studio would be graded solely on the quantity of work they produced. All those on the right side of the studio would be graded solely on the quality of the work they produced. His procedure was simple: on the final day of class he would bring in his bathroom scales and weigh the work of the 'quantity' group. Fifty kg of pots got an A-rating, forty kg of pots got a B-rating and so on. The group that was rated on quality, however, needed to produce only one pot that was as perfect as possible, to get an A-rating.

Three months later, when the teacher got down to grading, he noticed an interesting phenomenon. The works of the highest quantity group had produced higher quality pots than the higher quality pot group itself. That's because while the 'quantity' group was busily churning out piles of work and learning from their mistakes, the quality group had sat theorizing about perfection, and in the end had little more to show for their efforts than grandiose theories and a pile of clay. You can be a beginner in creating content, but with consistency and a high volume of content churned out, the quality of your content will improve over time. This is a journey experienced by most creators. Ira Glass, an American radio personality, shared this powerful quote that illustrates this point clearly:

'Nobody tells this to people who are beginners, I wish someone told me. All of us who do creative work, we get into it because we have good taste. But there is this gap. For the first couple of years you make stuff, it's just not that good. It's trying to be good, it has potential, but it's not. But your taste, the thing that got you into the game, is still killer. And your taste is why your work disappoints you. A lot of people never get past this phase, they quit. Most people I know who do interesting, creative work went through years of this. We know our work doesn't have this special thing that we want it to have. We all go through this. And if you are just starting out or you are still in this phase, you gotta know it's normal and the most important thing you can do is do a lot of work. Put yourself on a deadline so that every week you will finish one story. It is only by going through a volume of work that you will close the gap, and your work will be as good as your ambitions. And I took longer to figure out how to do this than anyone I've ever met. It's gonna take a while. It's normal to take a while. You just gotta fight your way through.'[34]

More business owners and marketers need to get comfortable with allowing others to know what you are up to in work. No matter who you are or what you do, your job is to tell your story and documenting it is the way to start. If you want your consumers to start listening to you, you need to show up. There are a lot of businesses out there that aren't producing enough content to build their influence. Too many of us think we only have one shot at success and we need to create the highest quality content that is beautifully designed and produced. What they don't realize is that the hunger to make the perfect piece of content is what's actually crippling them. If you want to be seen or heard in the online space, you have to put out valuable content on a regular basis.

Get Comfortable with Documenting

Gary Vaynerchuck advises his followers to document instead of create. What he means by that is to document the process of the work that you do. It is much more fruitful for you to talk about your process than about the actual advice you 'think' you should be giving to your audience. People who are willing to discuss their journeys instead of trying to look 'prim and proper' are going to win. The creative of how beautiful your content is subjective; beauty is in the eye of the beholder. Share what you're doing with your followers and engage them to be a part of your journey. Show them the behind-the-scenes to the work you put out, the process. Starting is the most important part and the biggest hurdle that most people are facing. Too many marketers and

---

[34] Clear, J., *What every successful person knows, but never says*, (17 January 2023). https://jamesclear.com/ira-glass-failure

business owners get stuck on pondering and strategizing instead of creating. Most people are anxious about how their content is going to show up even before creating the content.

Creating content·has become essential for the personal brand that entrepreneurs leverage to grow their business. It has become a part of marketing that cannot be left ignored. If you're not sure where to begin, don't worry. It's actually pretty simple. Whatever you love to talk about, talk about that. Even if one person finds it interesting, you've got something. Remember, even the most successful people in business started off as nobodies. Gary Vaynerchuck himself was not active on the internet until he hit 30 years of age and started Wine Library TV. Whatever it is that you love, talk to the world about it.

The truth is that most people are not good enough to make the content they want to be making. I know that's hard to digest, but it is true. The problem is that most individuals are focusing too much on their flaws and not maximizing their potential to win. In creating content, talent and skills matter. The quality of your content is really important. You can't just make a video about 'why you like to travel' and become a travel influencer someday. Your content needs to have depth. It needs to deliver value and resonate with a specific audience as opposed to being fluffy and for the masses. It's about depth, not width. You need to know what is going on in the world you are trying to be a part of? How can you insert yourself into the conversation? How aware are your consumers about you and your brand? All of these questions need to be properly addressed when you embark on a marketing strategy. To create high quality content, you need to start off with relevance. Here's a quote and a picture that really drives this message home.

The Only Way to Grow with Content Creation Is to Make Content That People Want to Consume.

When I heard that quote from my friend who had over 50,000 subscribers on Instagram and YouTube combined, I felt like a ton of bricks hit me. Because I had this sudden realization that I was approaching content creation from a different vantage point up till this point. For the longest time, I was sharing content about what I wanted to say. Never did I really look into finding out what my audience would be really interested to learn. That's when the focus shifted for me. Now, I follow the 80:20 rule when it comes to who I create content for. 80 per cent of the content I create is based on what my audience is interested in and the rest 20 per cent is based on what makes me tick. I don't believe it's either or because we are human beings and there are different aspects to us. So for me, the ratio is 80:20 but the ratio for you can be 50:50 or 10:90. It really depends on your industry and your audience. At the end of the day, if your content is relevant and useful, people will consume it.

> 'When consumers hear about a product today, their first reaction is 'Let me search online for it.' And so they go on a journey of discovery: about a product, a service, an issue, an opportunity. Today you are not behind your competition. You are not behind the technology. You are behind your consumer.'
>
> — Rishad Tobaccowala, Chief Strategy & Innovation Officer VivaKi

The Searcher

When you create content that people want to consume, you are essentially creating content for the searcher because they are the ones who have an intent. They have the intent of researching to learn more about the product or service. So when they do come to you, they are hot buyers who are ready to buy. This is similar to people who walk into your store or find you through Google and give you a call. The challenge with searchers is that they don't only search for you. They search for your competitors and compare options. You have to be the leader in pricing, quality and niche to stand out. The reason we see many entrepreneurs build up their presence on Google and YouTube is because it is a search-based platform i.e. people who are searching can find you easily. It makes it easier for them to get spotted, but there is no guarantee that the people who find you will see you as the best option for them because competition is fierce.

The Scroller

When you are very clear on the people you need to target, you can interrupt them with your ads. You can grab their attention and intrigue them to learn more by getting in touch. This way, you no longer have to wait around for someone to look for you. You have to plant desires in the minds of your dream customers. For this to work, you must know the interests of your target audience. You have to become good at hooking them and reeling them in. If you don't understand the core desires of your customers, then this technique will cause you to lose a fortune in marketing spend if you were to run ads. It is a better idea to hop on to this option once you are crystal clear of the psychographics of your customers. This is why social media agencies exist. They understand the platform, and they rely on you to understand your customer for the campaign to work well. If you don't understand your customer well, no amount of interruption marketing will bring in sales for you. Don't blame the agency. You as the marketer have to take full responsibility. In both cases, be it organic content or ad creative, quality is key.

Quality Trumps Everything

There's a simple way to find out if you've created quality content. If you ever worried that your content isn't good enough, or if you've ever poured your heart and soul into creating a piece of content only for it to get a few likes, comments and downloads? If so, don't worry because you're not alone. All content creators who are successful now have experienced this. They create their best piece of content, publish it, sit back and hope it takes off on its own to become a viral hit. When that doesn't happen, they feel discouraged, unmotivated, and they feel like giving up. Trust me, I've been there, and I know how it feels. Most people think that creating content that spreads is all about what you create, how great your information is, how in-depth it is compared to your competitor's content. Yes, these things matter. You can't put together garbage and expect it to resonate with people. You still need to craft your best content if you want to get ahead. But it's not enough to just create content that you think is good enough. You need to create content that people want to share and talk about. To achieve this result, you need to incorporate these psychological principles into your content to push the right buttons in your audience. The key is to create content that strikes a balance between what people want and what people need. What matters the most is if your content is leveraging the psychology of what makes people consume, comment and share your content. Here are the psychological principles.

1. Practical

You can post one, two, or even three times a day on social media and will still struggle to see results if your content is not useful. How do you make your content useful? The easiest way to is to teach your audience something they can take action on and see results. It can be content that makes people feel something or that leaves them with a great story or makes their whole day a little bit better. Jonah Berger, the author of the book, *Contagious*, discovered that practical content is often more viral than impractical content. That's great news, because to create useful content, you don't have to be the number one expert in your field. Many people who are really knowledgeable are terrible at explaining to others how they do what they do. There is a way to structure your content so that it is useful, interesting and people can understand it easily. Being truly helpful is way more valuable than just pushing information at people.

2. Authority

Here's the strange thing about authority. Most people think you need to be in a position of power to communicate with authority but this couldn't be further from the truth. According to Olivia Fox in her book, *The Charisma Myth*, authority has less to do with the influence you really have and more to do with whether your behaviour matches that of someone who is confident and influential. It's not what you say, it's how you say it with authority. There are ways to convey authority by building it into the structure of your content without sounding like you're bragging. Some people don't feel they are qualified to talk about their topic even though they provide the services that have produced results. Usually, it is because they have a black or white metric where they think they have to be the best in the topic to be qualified to speak about it. It's almost as if they fear the top person in their industry will hate on their content because they haven't dominated the market. Others wait till they have all their ducks in a row to get started and many are afraid to be called out as a scammer or a fraud. The imposter monster is real and it can cause a lot of fear in the minds of entrepreneurs.

Here's the thing: You don't need to be the number one in your industry to create content. You just need to be a few steps ahead of your peers. One of the biggest realizations I had in my entrepreneurship career was that I don't need to be a sixty year old to coach someone who's sixteen. In fact, being a twenty two year old back then, I was better placed to coach them than a sixty year old. As long as you can solve problems for your clients and you are more knowledgeable than them, you can position yourself as an authority.

You can also be a role-based expert where you document your journey as you learn through your experience. You share your mistakes candidly and people resonate with your journey. This can be done on social media and people see you as an expert.

The last form of authority is becoming a research expert. This is the expert that collects all the information and shares it with everyone. If you see the podcast interviews from Lewis Howes or Ali Abdaal, you will notice a number of experts on their shows sharing valuable information. A lot of top podcast owners share their own content but are valued more for being a super connector. Being surrounded by experts makes you an authority in your space. Incorporating the content of experts will make your content stand out as well .Check out my free resources guide at www.vivekiyyani.com/free for the worksheets and templates on embedding authority into your content.

3. Curiosity

Like it or not, curiosity has to be baked into every single piece of content you create. Curiosity is another one of those human behaviours we can't escape. When we hear only a part of the story, we can't help it, we want to know the ending. Professor George Loewenstein who studies curiosity at Carnegie Mellon University defines it as an innate human behaviour that's triggered when people feel there is a gap between what they know and what they want to know. He calls this the information gap and these are powerful because they get people to take action. Humans have the innate desire to close information gaps as a way to satisfy our curiosity. Here's why this is important for you to embed curiosity into all of your content. If you want your audience to take action i.e. make micro commitments, buy your products or join your email list, you can use information gaps to your advantage. Think of these information gaps as cliffhangers. It is easily seen on many top Netflix shows where they tease you with a little bit of information and then leave you hanging. This invokes curiosity and gets people pumped to watch the next episode and ensures higher viewership.

4. Identity

Have you ever had that feeling when you saw an ad where you think, wow, that's me! I remember watching the first GoPro commercial and thinking that because it encompassed the adventures I loved to take and it captured the moments I've lived. The ad connected with me personally because it connected with my identity. Identity is how you see yourself. It's how you want others to perceive you. It's who you are as a person. Your interests, motivations, dreams and goals make up your identity. It is the reason why some people are die hard Apple fans and Nike fans. You identify with certain brands. When someone consumes a piece of content, and thinks, 'Wow, that's me!' or 'I want to be that person the content is describing', it's because the content matches the individual's identity. On the flip side, when someone consumes a piece of content and hates it, that's also the identity trigger at work. It's seen as an identity mismatch. People feel strongly about their identity. That's why your content should give them the opportunity to say, 'This is how I'm different from other people and allows me to be comfortable in my own skin and uniqueness.' It's a natural way that gets people to share your content. The reason Greta Thunberg has been able to raise awareness about environmental issues is not because she's a charismatic personality. Far from it. The main reason she gets to influence others is because she has identified with the issues of saving the environment and others who feel the same way, others who have the same values, join forces to amplify the message. That is why introverts, gamers, and artists all gather together. Chris Do is an entrepreneur and a designer. His identity attracts other like-minded artists and designers who want to learn from him.

5. Reciprocity

Reciprocity is a psychological rule amongst humans. It simply states that people often respond to positive actions with another positive action. People love to return favours. There's nothing wrong or shady about it. The key is to offer to help in a way that's actually helpful and not fake. The best way to invoke reciprocity is through partnerships. If you're someone who is a wedding photographer, it makes sense for you to partner up with event venues, wedding dress providers, wedding organizers, food caterers, and so on to create content. Promoting them will help you gain attention from a reciprocal point of view. The more you elevate them, the more they will want to elevate you as well. As a result, you both win from the content you put out. If you are able to add a lot of value in your content, people will reciprocate by referring you to people in need of your services, even if they themselves have not purchased anything from you before. Why is this the case? It is reciprocity in the making. The sense of gratitude is repaid by pushing opportunities your way so make sure you share content that is worthwhile.

6. Controversy

The last principle is controversy because as humans, we love conflict between two ideas. I emphasize the importance of having content that stands out from the rest. It is similar to, for example, having Biryani. We can buy Chicken Biryani from many places, but which Biryani location do we remember forever? The one that tastes the best. Despite all the different places that offer Biryani, there is always that one place that stands out because they are different. In the content that you create, you need to be able to stand out from the rest. And the only way to do that, is to be polarizing. The idea of polarization means to be able to take a stand, and defend it strongly. That also means, you are willing to get in the 'bad books' of people who don't agree with your point of view.

And that's okay. Because not everyone will agree with you. But the ones who do, are your true fans and followers. Besides, taking a stand is the job of a thought leader.

How else will you lead the way for others to follow?

It's more important to be polarizing than neutralizing.

When you are polarized, it becomes easier for you to disrupt the way people think. You have something unique to offer the world. Your point of view becomes differentiated. And you stand out from all that noise. It sounds simple, but it is not. Many are afraid. Many find it too risky. And many would rather be safe than sorry. In your industry, if you want to have a name for yourself, be polarizing. Be the guy or gal who challenges norms and ideas. And backs it up with facts and figures. Be different, and your content will take off. When someone disagrees, or when someone is willing to question conventional wisdom, we can't help but watch. And yet, when most people create content, they're so worried about ruffling feathers and they water their content down. They think doing this makes them more likable or accessible. Actually, when you remove all potential for controversy, you also make your content less shareable. People like people who are polarized, who take a stand, even if they disagree because it gives them an opportunity to share their own perspective. This benefits everyone. You have to show up differently from your competitors and the content you share has to incorporate that. Millennials are overwhelmed with information from all around the world. If your content isn't new and different, not only will it not create the right impression, it won't get much visibility either. Because if the content you share on your website and social media platforms are pretty much the same as what others are saying, why would anyone share them? They are not going to get any social currency from sharing something that their contacts have probably seen before. They won't comment on your content because they've consumed something similar before. No one will invite you to their podcasts or shows because you're saying what has been said before by others before you. There's no differentiation! If you want more visibility through your marketing, share the 5 per cent or 20 per cent that is different and unique to you.

When you are willing to take a controversial stand, everyone joins in the conversation. This brings people to your profile or website and it gets them to share your content. Just a word of warning, don't create controversy for the sake of controversy and don't burn any bridges by offending people for the sake of offending people. You should only take a stand for something you truly believe in. Your brand is at stake here so make sure you know your stuff when you put out content that is controversial. You have to be able to back up your claims or this might backfire on you. There's a way to create a productive controversy that starts an awesome discussion without taking people down.

Once you embed these psychological principles into your content, it becomes rich with value. It gets people to engage and comment and spread the word about your content. People don't want to see the same old content on the same old topics. They want a refreshing take, and baking these principles into your content helps you create high-quality content.

Does that Mean You Have to Give All Your Valuable Content Away?

There's a difference between free content and paid content. One thing I learnt about content years back from a mentor of mine is that I was giving away too much of my paid content for free. This usually comes in the form of 'how to' and 'tutorial'-based content. This is a mistake in many ways. As business owners, we think that is the best way to help our audience get their desired results. The truth is a lot of people who have accessed your content have a lot of blind spots in their thinking. They have a lot of unresolved objections, limiting beliefs and lack the foundational knowledge. So when you teach them the 'how to' content, they are not going to be able to retain that information. As a result of that, prospects who do try out your 'how to' content don't get the desired results they were hoping for and then they blame you for misleading them. They conclude that your content isn't of high quality and it doesn't work for them. That's why you have to differentiate your free content from your paid content.

Information vs Transformation

Here's a caveat: If the only thing you sell is information i.e. courses or something along those lines, giving away everything might not be in your favour. However, if you are like Russell Brunson, who sells a software subscription service, 'giving away' books for a postage fee might be a worthwhile strategy to consider. The knowledge is not what you sell. It is the software. Similarly, if you have an implementation service or product that others can purchase, then giving away the information makes sense. With your free content, you can talk about the what and the why to help prospects uncover their blind spots. Giving them the 'lightbulb moments' will be of more value as opposed to giving them all your highly valued strategies and tactics. More often than not, they don't have the right mindset, skillset or toolset to execute on your strategies that will empower them to get the results they desire. The goal of your free content is to generate demand, not lower it. So don't give it all away if you only sell information products! You put in too much effort and time for you to give everything away for free. Give information for free if you have implementation products or services. Otherwise, don't give it all away.

Evergreen vs Temporary Content

Another key principle for you to take note when you create content, is to make sure it is evergreen content. In other words, it doesn't disappear into a black hole a few days after you post it. Have you noticed the amount of effort it takes for you to scroll through Facebook, Instagram, or TikTok to find that one post that you wanted to revisit? It's like a finger marathon when you think about it. Now, if you, the creator of your own content, gets tired trying to retrace that piece of content, how frustrated would your followers be if they can't find what they are looking for. It's akin to looking for a needle in a haystack, and can become very time consuming. In a world where people have short attention spans, no one prefers to doom scroll to find something. That's why it's important for you to make it as easy for your audience to consume the content that they will benefit from the most. Facebook allows you to pin a top post, Instagram and TikTok allow you to pin three posts, LinkedIn allows you to feature as many posts as you want on the top of your profile. The reason these platforms allow this is because they know that the average consumer has a short attention span of eight seconds or lesser. Typically featured content like this include videos, podcasts, articles, or webinars etc. Of course you want to have these on your website, or at least your website should be linking to the content for the user to find the content. Most content that you put out as a post on these social media platforms depreciate so fast over a short period of time. The moment you post a piece of content, after a few weeks, it becomes a struggle to find it again and there are no chances for it to reappear on anyone's newsfeed. The key is to establish permanence of your best content on your profile so that it becomes easy to find.

That's why I didn't go all-in on Clubhouse, a social media app that sprung up in April 2020, amidst the Covid-19 pandemic. It was the first audio-only social media app out there. There was a lot of hype with people talking about it on Facebook, Instagram and LinkedIn. To get in, you had to get an invite from someone who already had an account. This strategy brought hundreds of thousands of people into the platform. Plus it was only available for iPhones. In mid-February 2021, they hit their first big milestone of 10 million users. That's quite impressive for an app that's only been around for less than a year and exclusive to iPhone users. Fast forward to now, Clubhouse is missing in action. It's barely talked about on any of the social media platforms and people have moved on.

The thing about Clubhouse is that it is difficult to browse for something that interests you because all conversations on it are live. Nothing is recorded. Which means you always have to listen in to a conversation for a period of time before deciding if it's worth joining the room. That process of tuning in and then tuning out became a chore for people. Plus you had to take a lot of time out to listen to it without an immediate return on investment. For business owners and entrepreneurs, it provided no value to them in terms of creating digital assets. The conversations in the rooms were not recorded and could not be leveraged to build relationships with their audience. Everything was temporary and as my teacher used to say, 'carried away with the wind'. Creating content is one of the best ways to duplicate yourself if you don't have a marketing team under you. It becomes your salesperson, adding value to your audience, answering their questions and helping them out with their problems. That's why it is seen as an asset because it lifts a considerable amount of workload from you and saves you both time and effort that sometimes goes into repeating yourself over frequently asked questions.

Long-Form vs Short-Form Content

Millennials love short-form content. With their low attention span and urge to multi-task, short-form content is fast and easy to digest and easy to consume. Short-form content can be informative and educational but relying on short-form content alone will not help your audience to get to know you and your brand better. Short-form content is too short to help consumers understand deeply. It is simply digging at the surface level which can leave them feeling dissatisfied. It helps them learn a lot, but they've only learnt surface-level content. Going deeper is difficult and it is harder to create. You can pique interest for your audience to click the URL in your social media profile and then listen to the long form content. Short form content is really great to generate attention and curiosity. All the social media short-form content is merely a gateway to the longer form content and vice versa. At the end of the day, you want to bring your oblivious consumer and afflicted consumer to consume more high level, in-depth, long-form content, which I can understand, can be difficult to create.

Yet, anything worth doing is difficult, and deeper knowledge is often a part of that process, especially when you want to change or innovate. The good thing about long form content is that you can retrieve short form content from it. If you write blogs, shoot videos, or record podcasts, workshops or lectures, you definitely milk long form content to create shorter-form content. You can create more thirty-second videos, LinkedIn posts, carousel posts or infographics as a summarized version of your long form content. All you need to do is give the long form content to an editor to make a shorter piece of content from it. This way, you can leverage the algorithm while it still favours short-form content like vertical videos. Short-form content is the spark that gets you to care about something whereas long-form content is what gives you a deeper understanding of the subject matter.

Short form content helps you hook people in and get their attention. Long form content allows you to build trust and a relationship with the people who consume your content. At the end of the day, whether you create long form content, short form content, or document your journey with your mistakes and pitfalls, the key is in creating the assets that generate demand. Once you have put out the content and you notice an uptick in demand or traffic from your content pieces, you can leverage that 'proven' piece of content by using it to run ads. If you want more people to know more about you, run ads to short form content and redirect them to your longer form content. If you are looking to build trust, run ads to your longer form content and make them an offer they cannot refuse. It is not enough to simply create content. You must ensure people know about it, otherwise, how will you generate demand for your products or services? You can have the cure for cancer but if no one knows about it, how will it benefit you?

Think about It

- Are you currently creating content that generates demand?
- Do you have a strategy for creating long form and short form content?
- Are your content pieces evergreen material that people can find by browsing your social media profiles or do they need to doomscroll and spend hours to find it?
- How are you leveraging long form content to create more short form content?
- Are you actively promoting your proven pieces of content to get more customers?

Chapter 7

Algorithm: The Hidden Force That Curbs or Catapults Your Visibility

Social Media is going nowhere but up. The more innovative and creative your content, the more likely a post is to start a trend or go viral. More and more, the creator economy and niche content are dominating with the global influencer marketing industry predicted to surpass $16 billion in 2023. Now that you've learnt how to build digital assets and repurpose them for social media, it's time to dive deeper into the most important thing that will help you grow on social media. That's right, I'm talking about the algorithm. Now I know you might be thinking, *Why bother about the algorithm if it's always going to be changing?* You're right, the algorithm will keep changing because these social media companies keep innovating and coming up with new features to get users hooked onto their platforms. See it as a wave that lifts all boats.

Creating a piece of content that the algorithm is pushing is like going with the current. It is like stepping on an escalator to get to the next floor instead of climbing all the steps. I'm not saying you should forget everything and do exactly what the algorithms determine, and at the same time, ignoring the algorithm completely isn't the best move either. You have to find your sweet spot, and find a way to make it work so that you enjoy the content you create as a business owner or marketer and you also see the results. I know how demoralizing it can be to put in hours to create a piece of content only to realize that your audience didn't find much value in it. Sadly, that's how the market works; so your best bet is to do the things that also give you a lift. Otherwise, you will find yourself losing out to your competitors who are leveraging the algorithm to grow their follower base and generate more leads, appointments or sales.

For some marketers, they're like the little data puzzles just waiting to be solved. It is a great 'unknown' that is holding your content down. There is a ton of content floating around in the social media space. Without these algorithms, sifting through all the content on an account-by-account basis would be impossible. Algorithms do the legwork of delivering what you want and weeding out what you don't. There is also the belief that algorithms exist to push brands to pay a premium for social ads. If the brands cannot reach their audience organically, then turning to ads becomes the next logical step. Obviously, this means more money for these social media networks. Networks are traditionally vague about the specifics of their algorithms and understandably so. Marketers typically look at algorithms as roadblocks to achieving high visibility.

Each social media platform has its own native language and rules that are determined by its algorithm. When you understand the native language of these platforms, you get to grow the leverage you get from such platforms. Think of each platform as a country on its own. The people who hang out in the different countries follow different cultural norms, rules and decorum. Being aware of the nuances works in your favour.

So let's dig in.

Understand the Rules of the Game

Here's the thing about algorithms. They change fast. Very fast. In fact, what I write about algorithms today may not be relevant by the time you are reading this. That's just the reality of how quickly things change in the digital world. But does that mean you should ignore the algorithms? Absolutely not. The reason I am writing this chapter is to help you raise awareness of the bias that exists on digital platforms. Algorithms run the game. They are the rules. When you learn the rules, you stand a better chance at winning the game. Many of us are on different social media platforms for different purposes. For example, we may use Facebook to stay in touch with our family, Instagram to share pictures and behind-the-scenes with friends, YouTube for long form entertainment or education, LinkedIn for professional content and the news, and TikTok for short-form entertainment and education. This may vary for many of us. Each platform has its own set of features and rules. Each platform has its own positives and negatives.

Social media algorithm is a set of mathematical rules and data that make decisions about what users want to see on the platform. The social media sites create unique algorithms for every person who uses the site which means no two people will have the exact same social media newsfeed. In social media, algorithms help maintain order and assist in ranking search results and advertisements. With over 57 per cent of the world's population on social media, it is a massive undertaking to manage and monitor. This is why algorithms are so crucial in determining the validity and placement of social media accounts and content. Social networks prioritize which content a user sees in their feed by the likelihood that they'll actually want to see it. With so many users on the platform there's a need to create order and relevancy, and an algorithm does just that.

Before the switch to algorithms, most social media feeds displayed posts in reverse chronological order so the newest post showed up first. These platforms take the rein of determining which content to deliver based on your behaviour. The purpose of the algorithm is to filter our irrelevant content or content that's not high quality. This puts your content at risk of being buried or hidden from feeds if it does not fit the criteria. As a marketer, this means you need to have a constant pulse of the criteria that these social media platforms push out. These algorithms analyze user behaviour and interactions to surface content that is most relevant to each individual user. There are several types of algorithms. Some are chronological in nature, where the content is displayed in reverse chronological order, relevance based in nature, where the content is ranked based on how relevant it is to the user. Hashtags usually play a role in the categorization of content. Hybrid algorithms combine chronological and relevance based factors.

The reason why marketers look into algorithms is because of their impact on reach. Social media algorithms have greatly reduced organic reach for businesses and other content creators. To improve visibility, businesses can optimize their content for the platform's algorithm by creating high-quality, engaging content that resonates with their target audience. Artificial Intelligence and machine learning are playing an important role in social media algorithms as these technologies enable platforms to analyze vast amounts of data and make accurate predictions about what content will be most relevant and engaging to users.

Plus they are constantly evolving, so the marketers have to constantly adapt to them by experimenting with content and changing up marketing strategies. Social media algorithms vary by platform and depending on which platform you use the most, it's a good idea to understand what triggers the algorithm to push out your content versus limiting it.

TikTok Algorithm

While TikTok was already gaining popularity around the world, the Covid-19 pandemic has turbocharged its growth as a social media platform over the last two years. According to market intelligence firm Sensor Tower, global downloads of the app surged from 200 million in the last quarter of 2019 to more than 300 million in the first three months of 2020, when the pandemic saw consumers drawn to their mobile devices more than ever. TikTok got 690 million monthly visitors worldwide in May 2022. The platform received 1.766 billion visits that month with an average session duration of 03:48s.

TikTok is a pure vertical video platform and its 'For You' feed presents a stream of videos curated to each user's interests, making it easy for a user to find content and creators they love. So instead of one 'For You' feed for over one billion monthly active users, there are a billion 'For You' feeds tailored to what each user watches, likes and shares. This feed is powered by a recommendation system that delivers content to each user that is likely to be of interest to that particular user. The recommendations are based on a number of factors such as:

- User interactions such as the videos they like or share, accounts they follow, comments they post, and content they create
- Video information which might include details like captions, sounds, and hashtags
- Device and account setting like their language preference, country setting, and device type

The 'For You' page recommendations usually pull videos posted within the last ninety days. Most people think you need to sing and dance to succeed on TikTok and those who follow you are mostly teenagers. While this may be how they started, more and more individuals from different age groups are getting on board this platform. The app successfully reads user preferences and suggests perfect content while providing a wider reach for content generators because the algorithms prioritize content over the number of followers a user may have. TikTok's 'come as you are' culture where its creators can post casual videos of themselves at home allowed these influencers to continue producing content on a different platform without impacting their other personas or branded identities on other sites such as Instagram, Facebook, or YouTube. The isolation during the pandemic also gave older, Millennial influencers who were in their thirties to forties the time to learn how to use TikTok and overcome the inertia against using a new app. The algorithm takes into account how far a user got in the video, and whether or not they watched it in its entirety. Watching a video from beginning to end is a strong sign of interest and carries greater weight in the TikTok algorithm than the other contributing factors.

The number of total followers an account has does not result in their posts surfacing higher, or more often, based on the functionality of the 'For You' algorithm. Naturally, those who have a higher number of followers will have more overall visibility, but their posts are not given preferential treatment based on their popularity. Your track record of high-performing versus low-performing videos also do not affect placement. So you don't have to have a proven track record of producing viral content in order to get your videos showcased by the algorithm. A good piece of content is what the algorithm is looking for as opposed to the track record of the creator.

The 'TikTokification' of Social Media

TikTok recommends content based on the user's interests, rather than accounts they follow. This has left the other platforms scrambling to catch up, with the latest tweaks to its algorithm mimicking that of TikTok to beat TikTok at its own game. Snapchat introduced Spotlight, YouTube introduced Shorts, and Instagram introduced Reels—all to compete with TikTok. So why do so many apps copy TikTok's short video format? It's because they see the massive popularity of TikTok and they want some of that for themselves. As TikTok de-emphasized content based on posts from connections and replaced it with posts based on the 'reading' of the individual's preference, it shook up the way social media algorithms have been functioning in the other apps. That's because social media was initially a place where you went to see what was going on with people you knew and people you were interested in. This means that users will not only see posts from accounts they follow, but also from accounts they do not. The basic assumption was that you would always be most interested in those closest to you, and the algorithms focused on delivering their content in your newsfeeds. However, TikTok has shaken up that basis as its algorithm has shown that people can and will engage with content that is created by strangers, but is of their preference. Ultimately, all social media platforms are geared towards having as many users as possible, and having those users spend as much time as possible engaging within the platform. That's why we see older platforms push out more videos and infographics because they appeal to the Millennial generation as opposed to hyperlinks to news reports as preferred by older users. Facebook has tweaked its algorithm so that people scrolling through the home page can discover content that is uniquely personalized to them. In 2016, Instagram announced that user's feeds would prioritize 'the moments you care about', ending the reverse-chronological feed in favour of a curated one.[35]

Leveraging for Maximum Exposure

Start with a TikTok Pro account as it gives you access to reports. These reports tell you when your audience is most engaged. You can find this under the 'Follower Activity' report in the Follower tab. By analyzing this report, you can discover what your audience considers high quality content, that helps you create more higher quality content. TikTok also curates the videos on its platform based on specific hashtags that a user frequently engages in. It provides a layout of its community guidelines that sets the standard of what is and what isn't allowed on the platform. Just search 'Community Guidelines—TikTok' to get access to this. Now given the platform is predominantly a video platform, you only have three seconds to hook your viewer in. That's where you have to experiment with different captivating hooks to get and keep your viewers' attention. TikTok now allows you to create videos for up to 10 minutes, in a move to keep more users on its platform. On top of having an exciting hook to reel viewers in, put in effort to write clever captions. TikTok is known to have a feature that automatically adds captions for TikTok videos which has shown an improvement in social media engagement and overall discoverability amongst users. This promotes inclusivity for those who are deaf and Millennials are all about diversity and inclusion, so make sure it is reflected in the way you post your content! Lastly, this goes without saying by the way, increase your visibility and video shareability by using effects as they have the greatest impact due to their popularity among the user base. Filters and effects are used to make your video more compelling and engaging for viewers. Its vast library of effects and filters is what sets it apart from its

---

[35] Navene Elangovan, 'The Big Read: Watch out Facebook (and the world), as pandemic-fuelled TikTok boom unleashes the good, bad and ugly', *M Today*, (13 August 2022). https://www.todayonline.com/big-read/facebook-and-world-pandemic-fuelled-tiktok-boom-unleashes-good-bad-and-ugly-1968086

counterparts. If Facebook, Twitter, LinkedIn, and Instagram are the seniors in class, TikTok is considered the new kid around the block.

LinkedIn Algorithm

LinkedIn is known as the largest professional network and they have the numbers to prove it. With over 774 million members in more than 200 countries and territories, LinkedIn is one of the most popular social media platforms, offering job-seekers, businesses, and professionals the opportunity to connect on a global scale. About forty million people use LinkedIn to search for jobs each week and 40 per cent access it on a daily basis, totaling up to over one billion interactions per month. All in all, LinkedIn gives brands the opportunity to connect with a diverse and unique demographic. What's interesting about LinkedIn is that it has a 'Social Selling Index' (SSI) that measures how effective you are at establishing your professional brand, finding the right people, engaging with insights, and building relationships. According to LinkedIn, a higher SSI boosts a user's posts closer to the top of their feeds for individual user's posts. There are four categories in determining your 'Social Selling Index':

1. Establish your professional brand
2. Find the right people
3. Engage with insights
4. Build relationships

They all have a score out of twenty-five which totals to 100 and this score gets updated daily based on your activity. So just because you scored 83 per cent in January doesn't mean you won't score 65 per cent in May. Your score fluctuates based on your activities.

Leveraging for Maximum Exposure

In order to maximize your efforts by engaging on LinkedIn, you have to know how LinkedIn works. There are three ranking signals that the LinkedIn algorithm uses to rank posts in a user's feed.

1. Law of Three Degrees

You can have up to 30,000 1st connections on LinkedIn. These are the individuals that you have connected with. The larger your 1st connections, the more 2nd connections and 3rd connections you will have. It is highly recommended that you actively make an effort to connect with individuals who will be useful to have in your network. But that's because LinkedIn eventually wants you to pay for their premium account. In reality, the more people you connect with, the more opportunities you will attract. That means, even if you have an invite from a bikini model on LinkedIn, you will benefit from the connections you get in the second and third degree as a result of connecting. However, that doesn't mean you need their bikini photos to show up on your LinkedIn feed. To avoid that from happening, simply unfollow them. You get the connections without embarrassing yourself as their bikini photos will not show up on your LinkedIn feed.

As of 2019, LinkedIn started deprioritizing content from mega influencers like Bill Gates and Richard Branson and instead began highlighting content from users' personal connections. That means you don't need to be an influencer with a lot of followers to get your posts visible to more people. The more connections you have, the better visibility you get. Users typically see posts by people they engage with often, as well as by anyone who posts consistently. Users also see more posts from connections with whom they share interests and skills based on their LinkedIn profile.[36]

2. Interest Relevance

LinkedIn uses what is known as an 'interest graph' to augment the personal connection signals and knowledge graph. The interest graph represents relationships between LinkedIn users and a number of

---

[36] Tim Jurka, 'A Look Behind the AI that Powers LinkedIn's Feed: Sifting through Billions of Conversations to Create Personalized News Feeds for Hundreds of Millions of Members', *Linkedin Engineering*, (29 March 2018). https://engineering.linkedin.com/blog/2018/03/a-look-behind-the-ai-that-powers-linkedins-feed--sifting-through

topics. This lets LinkedIn measure how interested users are in certain topics, how related topics are to one another and which connections share a user's interests. The algorithm also looks at the companies, hashtags, the people, and topics mentioned in a post. The algorithm looks at the power hour, which is the first hour in which you launch a post, to see the amount of attention it attracts. It fires up your post to fifty random individuals and if that gains some likes and comments, the algorithm continues to serve your content to even more people in your first, second and third network. However, if you don't get much engagement, it will kill your post i.e. not many people will get to see it. LinkedIn is also known to punish your posts if you put external links to other platforms or websites in your post. When I say punish, what I mean is that it limits the visibility of your posts. The simple reason being, they want to keep you on LinkedIn for as long as possible. This applies to all platforms, not just LinkedIn. Even if the pictures you post are of low pixel quality, it will reduce your reach.

3. Engagement Probability

Interaction plays a big role in a post's ranking on LinkedIn. The platform uses machine learning to rank interactions based on how likely a user is to comment on, share, or react to a post based on the content and people they have interacted with in the past. They also look at how quickly a post starts receiving engagement, especially within the first hour, after it is published. The faster the user starts interacting in a post, the more likely it is to show up at the top of others' feeds. As a user comments regularly on others' posts in the LinkedIn feed, they're more likely to see interactions on their own content, which in turn pushes them up on other people's feeds. This is something that marketers need to understand. If you want to build a warm relationship with individuals you want to connect with, you will have to engage with them via their posts. Put out thoughtful comments, share stories, and add value to their conversation.

The more engagement you give, the more engagement you will get. Over time, the person you intend to connect with will have warmed up to you to accept your connection and perhaps even get on a call to learn how you can work together. A lot of individuals don't understand this basic concept of engaging with people before making the connection and I don't blame them. Most people have a LinkedIn account but they aren't active on it. They don't like, comment or post anything for the marketer to interact with them. This just means that there are a lot of individuals who are silently watching in the shadows like a fly on the wall. In such cases, it is indeed a challenge to build a relationship with the person or get a chance to warm up to them before connecting with them so don't feel bad if the individual you are targeting is a passive user. Focus instead on the individuals who are active and engage with their content.

In the event you get a troll on your post, you can decide to leverage his comments to raise the visibility of your post. For every comment he posts, instead of defending yourself, you can ask questions to get him to explain his hateful comment. This is good because you can remain professional, get more views on your post and at the same time, it allows others to chime in and contribute to the topic of the post.

4. Your Content Format

The role of formats also plays a role in triggering social media algorithms. Different content formats, such as images, videos, text, polls, and live streams, may be prioritized differently depending on the platform's algorithm. For example, Instagram was known to prioritize Reels for a long time over static images; so businesses that wanted to leverage this could improve their visibility simply by creating content in a format that the algorithm promotes. Similarly, LinkedIn promoted the 'Polls' feature when it released it by giving it maximum exposure. Therefore, using the right content format can help increase engagement and improve a business's visibility on social media. It's important to note that the most important factor in triggering the algorithm is still the quality and relevance of the content in terms of entertainment or education.

Hot Tip

The good thing about LinkedIn is that it allows you to get notified if someone you follow is posting content. All you have to do is click the notification bell on their profile, and every post they put out will give you a notification. That is your reminder to engage with the person's posts to increase the familiarity. The more you comment on their posts, the more open they are to connecting with you on a deeper level. It might sound borderline stalker-*ish* but it is not, if it is done in the right fashion.

Make it a point to engage with comments on five to ten profiles before you post out new content. Your comments will notify the different contacts of your comments and it will increase the chances of your new post appearing in their newsfeed. Moreover, because you gave them the engagement, they are also more likely to give you the same engagement back. This is how relationships are built in the online space. Many B2B sales are done this way, where individuals connect and end up doing business with each other, which is what most businesses want anyway. Gone are the days where you connect with prospects and barrage them with a series of marketing and sales messages. Nobody likes to have offers shoved down their throats; so be wary of being aggressive in terms of marketing.

Another way to trigger the algorithm in your favour is to create content that is focused on your niche and your audience's specific interests. Members are known to be more interested in going deep on topics they are really interested in. Focusing on high quality content that helps professionals to succeed is mostly a win on LinkedIn as long as it is relevant to the industry. One of the key features that LinkedIn is pushing out is the polls feature. The more polls you do, the more engagement it gets because users only need to vote. It is your prerogative to ask interesting questions and collect useful insights from this feature. If you are sharing an industry insight, open up the conversation to your followers, and ask them to share their experiences on the topic. You can do this by tagging them to get their attention on the post. LinkedIn presents a unique opportunity for individuals and brands alike to reach influential decision makers across industries. The LinkedIn algorithm prioritizes engagement, relevance, and connection. Therefore, create content with your audience in mind.[37]

The 'Enshittification' of platforms

'How do social media platforms die? First, they are good to their users, then they abuse their users to make things better for their business customers; finally they abuse their business customers to claw back all the value for themselves. Then, they die.'

—Cory Doctorow[38]

'Enshittification' is a term used by Cory Doctorow, to describe a common problem that occurs when a platform, like a social media platform, makes it easy to change how it distributes value. These platforms act as a middleman between buyers and sellers and become increasingly greedy, taking a larger share of the value exchanged between them. In the early days, it gave its users a lot of traffic because it needed more users. Then, as its users increase, it slowly claws back on the traffic it gives users. This is what happened to Facebook.

In the early days, Facebook was good to you. It boosted your posts and showed you content that you craved. As a marketer, you're happy. You are getting the reach you desire and hitting all your marketing goals. So you continue with Facebook. Slowly, but surely, Facebook reduces the reach of your organic posts. At this point you're stuck. You can't leave the platform for another because it would mean you have to restart all over again. It would also be a near-impossible task to get your connections to jump ship to another platform with you.

Imagine the effort needed to persuade all your friends to leave Facebook just because your posts aren't getting the reach it used to. So essentially, you're stuck. You've built too much on this platform to simply start all over on another platform. This is when the platforms

---

[37] Tara Johnson, 'How the Linkedin Algorithm Works in 2023', *Tinuiti*, (25 January 2023). https://tinuiti.com/blog/paid-social/linkedin-algorithm/

[38] 'The "Enshittification" of TikTok', *Wired*. https://www.wired.com/story/tiktok-platforms-cory-doctorow/

turn the tide. They then your newsfeed with posts from accounts you never followed. Usually, these are media companies that need the traffic. Once these media companies are dependent on Facebook to drive traffic, Facebook cuts down on the traffic that flows to these publications. This is where the algorithm suppresses posts unless it is paid for and 'boosted'. Then, Facebook adds advertisements into the mix. Advertisers get a great deal and become hooked to the platform to drive profits. Over time, Facebook increases its prices for the advertisers. Eventually, the platform ends up giving minimal value to its users and advertisers. This is called 'enshittification'.

Using any platform for marketing can be like working for a boss that takes out money from your salary for all the mistakes you make, except, he doesn't tell you what mistakes you made. If you know the mistakes you made, you will naturally correct them.

Think about It

- Has the content you have been uploading on social media so far been adhering to the platform's algorithm preferences?
- What formats are you producing your content in? Which platform algorithms can push them out the furthest for your brand?
- How do you counter the algorithm bias for your own brand?
- How are you keeping on top of the algorithmic changes and trends?
- How can you leverage the ever-changing algorithms for your brand's visibility?

Chapter 8

ACQUIRE: Everything is Downstream from Lead Generation

In the previous chapters, we have been talking about the importance of creating content and digital media assets that help you to build a relationship with Millennials online. These assets are what they search for when they have a problem and when they do find really good content that educates and solves their problems, they become a fan. Now despite all of this, it's important to realize that content is NOT king.

Younger generations, specifically Millennials and Gen Zs, agree that an online presence is more important than a physical brick-and-mortar location for companies. They take that even further and believe that their online first impressions are more important than their real-world ones. Sixty-two per cent of Millennials said that they believe how a brand presents itself online is more important than how they present themselves in person. This is a significant leap from the 38 per cent of Gen X and 29 per cent of Baby Boomers who participated. Regardless of priority levels, digital has become an ubiquitous part of everyday life for everyone. It makes sense that this digital first impression holds such high importance when considering that majority of younger generations look up people before meeting them for the first time in person. Older generations do this as well, but to a lesser degree. This digital first impression extends to purchases in particular. A good percentage of all generations look up the websites of businesses before shopping or eating there. A well designed website made them more likely to shop in person, according to 70 per cent of the respondents.[39]

In the online world, you only have a tenth of a second to grab someone's attention. And during that time, people make snap judgements about you, your business and your website—before they read your content. According to Elizabeth Sillence, the research she did with her team proves this. They conducted a study where they asked a bunch of people to find websites about hypertension. Then she asked people to record whether they trusted or distrusted the websites they found, and why. Not surprisingly, when she reviewed the answers on why people distrusted the website, 94 per cent cited design as the issue. The study showed clearly that the look and feel of the website was the main driver of first impressions. At the same time, poor interface design was associated with rapid rejection and mistrust of a website. Similar results were found from research by Consumer WebWatch. They found that what people say about how they evaluate the trust of a website differs from how they really evaluate it. The data they collected showed that the average consumer paid far more attention to superficial aspects of a site, such as visual cues, than to its content. Every customer wants to feel that they're buying from an authentic, legitimate brand.

If a customer encounters a website with outdated design, broken links, and glaring pop-ups, they'll logically conclude the brand is also out of date and undesirable. A brand's first impression is strengthened by high-quality web design and navigation experiences. Make sure that the page loading times are as fast as possible.

The aesthetics need to be appropriate and generate a desire to read on. Bad design is used to weed out companies that don't understand user experience (UX). Visitors judge a site within the flash of a microsecond, long before they begin to read the words or watch the videos. In the

---

grand scheme of things, if you get your design all wrong, it doesn't matter what you say because no one will read it. The impression you make on them can either get them to remain on your page and learn more or leave your page and turn to a competitor.

A good design acts like a halo effect for the brand. Humans have cognitive bias and it is seen amongst people as well. People who are considered attractive tend to be rated higher on other positive traits as well. The halo effect makes it so that perceptions of one quality lead to biased judgements of other qualities. When you see someone through the lens of the halo effect, you are seeing them cast in a similar light. That 'halo' created by your perception of one characteristic covers them in the same way. One study even found jurors were less likely to believe that attractive people were guilty of criminal behaviour. Marketers are known to take advantage of the 'halo effect' to sell products and services. That's why celebrities are asked to endorse a particular item even if they hardly use it. The transference of the positive evaluation of the celebrity spreads to the product or service itself and that generates sales.

What's interesting to see is that this applies in the digital space, be it websites, landing pages or social media profiles. A study examined the effects of visual appeal and usability on user performance and satisfaction with a website. Users completed different tasks on websites which varied in visual appeal (high and low) and usability (high and low). The results showed that first impressions are most influenced by the visual appeal of the site. Users gave high 'usability and interest ratings' to sites with high visual appeal and low 'usability and interest ratings' to sites with low visual appeal. User perceptions of a low-appeal website were not significantly influenced by the site's usability, even after a successful experience with the website. That's why it's key to invest in design as it is the thing that matters most in pulling users in.

A decade ago, networking was all about first impressions. Everyone was very particular with how they looked, how they introduced themselves, and the people they connected with. Everything was strategic. In the physical world, the tactics are straightforward. All you needed was to smile, dress sharp, have a firm handshake, and be friendly. Online impressions are a different story altogether.

When the pandemic struck, people had no choice but to shift online. Now many of us work and socialize virtually more often than in person. The exception has turned into the norm. And unlike the physical world where you can only be at one place at one time, there are a lot of places you can be discovered online.

Your first impression is no longer made in person; it is made online.

The same goes for social media profiles and pages. All of them have a design element attached to it to give it your brand's look and feel. Having a consistent look and feel is important because it impacts how the audience perceives your brand. Whether you are logging onto a Zoom call or sending a message on LinkedIn, people will take note of your online appearance. Your brand has different digital records that impact how it is perceived. Facebook, Instagram, TikTok, LinkedIn, and other social media accounts are part and parcel of your online appearance. All your public posts add to your online brand and affect what consumers find when they search you or your brand.

Even your past work shows up online, including your public posts that you put up on social media. Even many big, successful companies that have become faceless organizations are starting to realize the importance of key people of influence at every single level of the organization. That means that some of the engineers might speak at conferences, some of the sales people might position themselves on panels and the media, and of course the CEO, the Chairman, and the board are out there having a voice. If you simply compare organizations like Porsche versus Tesla, Porsche is about more than ninety years old and it's a loved brand but if you ask the man on the street, who is the CEO of Porsche, who's on the board of Porsche, who are the engineers at Porsche, they wouldn't be able to tell you the answer. However, if you ask the same question about Tesla, which is only twenty years old, it's much easier to name their leaders and has a higher valuation than Porsche. The reason for its success is that the CEO is a very well-known individual, Elon Musk. He's an iconic entrepreneur and he's doing all sorts of things on the planet. He can pick up the phone and get in the media if he wants to, arrange appointments with other key people of influence, and that's incredibly valuable to the organization. As a brand, having more employees active online as ambassadors is beneficial to the organization. In such cases, it is also in the organization's interests to ensure their employees are supported to have a well-designed profile on their professional platforms.

Are Your Social Media Accounts Collecting Digital Dust?

I know of many friends who started out a LinkedIn account but left it at that. They created an account and never looked back. It is inactive and it is pretty obvious to an outsider that this account was never active. Nothing is more frustrating to Millennials than finding an account only to realize it hasn't been active in a long while. Forming an online presence is showing your consumers that you're engaged in digital acceleration.

If you are a small business owner or solopreneur, it is crucial for you to show up as the face of the organization. Having a personal brand will extend to the opportunities you receive for your business.

- Profile Picture
- Cover Photo
- Website Link
- Headline
- Featured Content

The Aim of Social Media and Websites

Millennials are everywhere. You can find them on all social media platforms. The difference purely is how many of them are concentrated in that particular platform. Naturally, you will notice that some platforms have more Millennials active compared to older generations. It's quite similar to Little India in Singapore. If you want to eat Indian cuisine, you can find it all over Singapore. However, you have a variety of options highly concentrated in Little India. If you are looking to capture more of the Millennial market, it only makes sense to put out even more content on the platforms that they frequent regularly. If you want to hunt for sharks you can't go to a lake or a pond to find them.

You have to venture out to the sea, where you can find them. Yet, I see so many business owners make this mistake when I get on a coaching call with them. Many know the importance of creating content on social media and for their websites, but very few have a clear cut strategy on how they can leverage content to generate leads, appointments or sales.

Very few business owners get actual results from their social media profiles and website with a positive return on investment. More often than not, the current website and social media platforms act as a painting on the wall. It looks good, but doesn't add much value to the business beyond that. That's why you hear many entrepreneurs grumble about social media and websites being a waste of time and money. Yeah, well if they don't understand the strategy behind these platforms, and merely have a website and social presence online because of FOMO, it is going to end up as a waste of resources. If you have zoned in on the target audience you are looking to work with but your conversions are zero or low, you need to understand the concept of micro-commitments.

The Power of Micro-Commitments

In marketing terms, a micro-commitment is a small, initial step that a potential customer takes towards making a larger commitment, such as making a purchase or signing up for a service. Micro-commitments are designed to build trust and familiarity with a brand, as well as to reduce the perceived risk of taking a larger action. Examples of micro-commitments include signing up for a newsletter, following a brand on social media, or downloading a free e-book. By engaging in these smaller actions, potential customers become more comfortable with a brand and more likely to eventually make a larger commitment. Micro-commitments are the key to conversions in this modern marketing landscape. If you have a high amount of traffic (visitors) and yet you are having trouble generating leads from your website, learning more about micro-commitments can help you solve this problem. As humans, we don't like to rush into commitments, especially if there's a lot at stake. Most of us are cautious before investing time and money and like to move slowly until we feel more informed to make a conscious decision.

Going back to my analogy of hunting for sharks, you need the right equipment to hunt for sharks. Having a boat and rowing out to the sea alone will not help you capture any sharks. You need bait and blood to reel them in. Social media content that you put out becomes the bait that gives consumers a reason to keep revisiting your page or your website. Your website is the hub and heart of everything else you do online. That means your website needs to accurately and professionally represent who you are since you won't be able to physically be there when someone is checking out your website. It not only has to look great, it has to be functional in helping your potential customers understand who you are, what you do, who you do it for, how you do it and what you want people who visit to do next.

However, the problem is many businesses ask for too big of a commitment too soon. It's like going out on a first date with a potential partner and asking her to marry you that instant. Your brain perceives change as a potential threat and the more significant the change, the more inertia that comes with it. They need to feel they can trust you and your products first. Getting to this stage takes time if your consumer is an oblivious consumer or an afflicted consumer. If you push consumers too hard or too quickly, you risk losing them forever to your competitors. Asking them to get on a sales call or asking them to fill out a 10-step form about themselves may seem too much of a commitment at their current stage. New visitors to your website probably don't know you or your brand at a personal level, and most people won't give you something precious unless they see the value or feel the connection. So it's natural for them to have a sense of skepticism and it is your job to ease that sense of skepticism through your content. It is highly likely that they may visit your website and social media pages several times before they make a micro-commitment to divulge their data. Of course, the higher the value of your freebie, or the more persuasive your offer, the higher the chances of converting your visitors faster. Once people are on your website, it is critical for you to convert them into an email following.

The reason is simple. Relying purely on social media is foolishness. Meta experienced its worst outage ever on 13 March 2019. The company's most popular apps, Facebook, Instagram, and WhatsApp all went down, affecting users around the globe. For business owners and marketers, it was a rude awakening that putting all their marketing eggs in one basket could cost them their business. Twenty-four hours later, Facebook gave the all-clear signal for us to get back to our regular scrolling of news feeds while business owners and entrepreneurs were left assessing the damage, trying to determine how much sales they lost during the outage. There's no denying that social media marketing is a solid business strategy when done right and paired with other marketing strategies and platforms. However, here's a reality check for you:

You Don't Own the Platform! One day I changed my password to my account and tried to log in. Facebook asked me to verify my details by asking me to key in the OTP that was sent via SMS. Except I never received any SMS. Despite my countless tries, I didn't get an OTP via SMS or via email and I didn't know how else to proceed. I tried searching the help section for details and went through multiple forums and even googled the issue, but to no avail. That's when I realized the importance of having direct access to my community instead of relying on a platform for it. Luckily, I have a close friend who is a super-connector and she had a friend at Facebook. She reached out, asked for a favour on my behalf, and the whole issue was sorted within a few hours. Talk about the power of your network, eh! To think I wasted all that time trying to figure it out myself. Now, if you were like me, what would you do if you lost access to your Facebook, Instagram, LinkedIn, or TikTok account overnight? Would it affect your business? Could you quickly move on or would you be left crying and paralyzed knowing you have no other way to connect with your audience other than to start from scratch, all over again?

The only way you can truly ensure you will not be held hostage by another social media platform outage or mishap is to have a diversified marketing strategy. Don't go all-in on these social media platforms without a solid backup plan. The best backup plan is to build your email list while you build your social media presence. It gives you a direct line of unfiltered communication between you and your audience. You own your email list. You don't own any of these social media platforms. You can switch marketing platforms in an instant if you have your email list with you but you can't do the same for your social media following. No matter how big your following on any of these platforms, or how much money you've spent on the platform, you do not own it, and you do not control what happens to it.

Building Your Email List

That's why it's critical to capture the basic contact details of your fans when they visit your website. When your consumers are on your website, you know they are either an afflicted consumer or an informed one. They may have found out about you through a variety of means, and when they are on your website, they are gathering information to decide if they really like your brand or not. Do they like the feeling they get from your website? Now even if they do like what they see, they may not be ready to make a purchase yet, especially if the products or services you offer are a high ticket item that is four figures and beyond. They might not even be ready to get on a call with you for that matter. This is your opportunity to capture the details of the website visitor so that you can continue to build the relationship with them by adding value through your emails. The more value you add by answering the questions in their mind, the higher the chance they lean towards you as a potential vendor for their needs and wants. Sometimes, you get informed consumers visiting your website and they're ready to commit to a call and make a purchase.[40]

In order to build your email list, all you really need is a form for them to fill up. A form that requires your consumers to fill out basic details like their name and email address at a minimum. Usually, the form comes with an exchange of value to entice the visitor to make a micro-commitment. Exchanging your contact details in return for

---

[40] Racquel, 'Why You Must Not Rely Alone on Social Media for your Marketing', *Better Marketing*, (4 February 2020). https://bettermarketing.pub/why-you-must-not-rely-on-social-media-alone-for-your-marketing-780c0572301e#:~:text=You%20Don'tpercent20Own%20the,ads%20account%20inpercent 20an%20instant.

something basic that you see of value is one way to generate leads from your website. This also allows the consumer to get to know you a little bit better through the emails you can send to them over time to nurture the relationship. It is not hard to say yes to something of high value—which happens to be free. It's the first major step to getting a larger commitment down the road.

How to Increase Conversions

Freebies like these are called lead magnets in the marketing world. A lead magnet is something that motivates a potential client to connect with you so that you can follow up with them. However, it has to be something that your audience finds valuable. It can come in a multitude of forms, like a scorecard, a report, a video, a checklist, a tool, etc. fifteen years ago if you offered a lead magnet you would probably be the few doing so and chances are you would have had a good conversion of the people signing up. Today, there are obviously a lot more lead magnets out there so it's important for you to have a really good idea of what your consumers really want.

Before we dive deep into the conversion strategies, it's important for you as the business owner to understand the journey customers take to become customers. A customer journey is simply a series of step by step actions from the moment somebody first hears about your business to the moment they become your biggest raving fan years down the line. Here's how it looks like with some sample answers:

How will a potential prospect hear about me?

- Through my books
- They might see my LinkedIn posts and articles
- They can find me through Google search
- Word of mouth
- My repurposed content on TikTok, Instagram, and Facebook
- Podcast Interviews

After they hear about your business, they will usually go to Google to learn more about you and your business. When people first land on this website, it is important for you to grab their attention by providing them with something that will excite them, in the form of a lead magnet. Then, as they scroll down on your website, it would be a good idea to have someone from your company welcome the visitor through a short video. Think of it as a door-greeter video which describes who you are, what you do for your clients, and what you want the visitor to do next on the website. It's important to immediately make a personal connection once someone lands on your website to allow people to get to know the real, authentic brand that you have built. This serves as a qualification process because those who like what they see, will lean in further and be more inclined to purchase from you whereas those who don't like what they see in the video will automatically disqualify themselves. That's perfectly okay, because you don't have to be all things to all people. Your vibe attracts your tribe and you want more of the ideal clients in your tribe. You don't want everyone to be your client because there is such a thing as a nightmare client. The video helps to attract the right people and repel the wrong people. At the end of the video, you have to tell the visitor what you want them to do next. It could be to go to another page or to opt in and download the lead magnet or to check out some piece of content. Whatever the case, you have to be clear about what you want the website visitor to do. Here's an example below:

What next three steps do I want the prospect to take on my website?

- Watch home page video
- Check out the free resources page
- Download whichever free resource they need the most

Even after they download the free resource, I share with them a video on what I want them to do next. It could be simple actions such as scheduling a call so that I can learn more about the visitor and what their needs are at the moment. Some visitors are event organizers who are looking for a speaker, and scheduling a call helps them make a better decision. Some visitors are solopreneurs, insurance agents, or business owners, who want help with coaching and content creation. The same call-to-action of scheduling a call helps me move them along the sales pipeline. By mapping out the customer journey and marking key actions for the visitors to take, you are drastically increasing the odds that somebody will take that journey with you. After they make some form of purchase with you, you can continue to guide them on the customer journey to buy the next thing that they need.

- How will a prospect hear about me?
- What next three steps do I want the prospect to take on my website?
- What next?

1. High-quality Lead Magnet

The best way to find out what lead magnet is good for your audience is by visiting the websites and social media pages of your competitors and see what they are being offered. Following that, you should make a note of what the lead magnet is in terms of the problems it is solving and what kind of results it is helping their audience to achieve. It is also a good idea to take note of the format of the lead magnet and how they are promoting it on their website and social media platforms. Upon tracking all of the above, you can then sit down to think about differentiating your lead magnet from your competitors. To confirm this is what your existing subscribers want, ask them to fill out the answer to this question:

What is your number 1 burning question when it comes to _____*?*

Your lead magnet needs to deliver on the promise. Whatever it is that your lead magnet says it is going to do, it has to add value, give insights, and help the consumer get the result that you've promised. You've probably signed up for some freebies on the internet which looked very attractive, you downloaded it, looked at it but you went *'Urgh, is that it?'* That kind of a lead magnet isn't very helpful in building a strong relationship with your prospects. Your lead magnet has to be irresistible and for it to be irresistible, it should fulfill these three criteria.

i) It Should be Insanely Practical

This means it should be useful and something that they can easily take action on. Forty-five ways to increase your productivity isn't really useful or easy to take action on. Instead, sharing something like 'The one strategy you can start using today to increase productivity' is much better.

ii) It Should be Specific

The more specific your free thing is, the more number of people will want to download it. It can either solve a specific problem, or it can address a specific type of customer. Ideally, it will solve a specific problem for a specific type of customer. For instance, imagine you run a general nutrition website and your target audience is mothers over forty. You can create a free thing specifically for busy moms over forty such as 'The one-week guide to get your family to spend more time together while eating healthily'. This solves a specific problem for a specific demographic. Something like this always converts better than typical lead magnets that say 'How to eat healthier in seven days?'

iii) It Should be Small

By small, I mean something like a one page cheatsheet, a mini ebook, a simple checklist, a basic template, a free lesson mini course or anything that's quick and easy to create. I've seen some of my friends in my network give away things before that have a thirty day video course on productivity and a six month course on how to grow your followers on Instagram for free. As much as I believe giving an insane amount of value is a good thing for all businesses, and it feels good to give it away, it's way too much information. Remember, your visitors are opting in for free and while it is a commitment, it is a micro-commitment. Giving away this much material is a surefire way to overwhelm people before they even know you have something to sell. Plus, your audience isn't ready for that type of full transformation yet. They just signed up! They are just beginning to learn about you and your brand. They're not ready to make such a huge commitment until they learn a little bit more about you.

The other reason why you want to keep your lead magnet small is because you want to test out these different lead magnet ideas. You need to ensure they resonate with people. You don't want to waste your time creating something for free only to find out no one was interested in that in the first place. You may have to test a few different ideas, so don't waste time on a huge lead magnet. Right now, you're simply looking to create something that is easy and quick to alleviate your customer's problems. Here is an example. Bidsketch is a software company that helps customers create professional client proposals in minutes. When you sign up for their email list, you immediately get a sample proposal. That's small, specific, and insanely practical.

You want your lead magnet to take your potential clients closer to wanting to work with you. If it lets them down or if it doesn't deliver on the promise, it's only going to take them further away. You want your lead magnet to build your company's credibility and trust so that they are closer to wanting to buy from your company and because of that lead magnet, you want them to look forward to receiving follow up emails anticipating the additional value they are going to get from you.

2. Online and Offline Community

If you don't have any content yet, you can still offer an online community for your potential clients where they can exchange ideas and help each other out. If you can make that community really valuable for members it can be a lead magnet and you'll find the members promoting it for you. Moreover, if your target audience are local individuals, you will find it easier to organize networking events and value-added workshops for them to be involved in the community. Moreover, because you are able to talk to them personally on a regular basis in person, it is an even better way to establish and nurture the relationship. There are many businesses where lunches and dinners are hosted by the business which then becomes a meeting point for current clients and potential clients. Having a networking event like this enhances the trust prospects have in working with you. Networking is always great for the attendees and they always learn something. Plus, there is no overt selling but it positions the hosts as leaders in the field and gives them the opportunity to follow up after the events.

3. Interview Them as a Guest

There are many consumers out there who love to get more visibility for themselves because it makes them look like an authority. One of the ways you can attract new consumers to get in touch with you and divulge their name and email address is to offer them a spot in your regular article, video, newsletter or podcast. The visibility and the exposure could be something that incentivises them to become a part of your community. This becomes an asset for you as well as for your prospect which they can also use in their own PR. When I was writing my first book *Empowering Millennials*, I reached out to many Millennials and interviewed them on their life goals and what's important to them. I then published their stories on LinkedIn as an article and they loved it. It was one of the ways that I grew my community. I did the same thing for my second book, *Engaging Millennials*, where I reached out to multiple HR leaders to interview them about their experiences with Millennials in their organizations. People love to be in the spotlight and they love it even more when you approach them as opposed to them having to reach out for a spot. As much as you do this with your prospects, do not forget to feature your existing clientele if they too show an interest to be featured. When they do get featured, they share the contents with their network which is an excellent way for others to learn more about you in a very subtle and discreet manner. Most importantly, you and your business stand out and you get noticed as a by-product of this.

While the examples I've used above might not work for all types of businesses in the exact same fashion, what's important for you to understand are the principles behind it. Start by thinking about what your potential clientele value and then think how you can offer it to them in a creative way. Not all lead magnets have to be the typical scorecard, report, video, checklist, or template. Anything you do at a reasonable cost will help you strengthen your relationship.

4. Optimizing Your Website for Conversions

The first thing to ensure when you want to increase the number of people signing up to your lead magnet is if the opt-in form is highly visible to the visitor. When you go to some websites, they don't even have an opt-in form, or they have one but it is hidden all the way down at the bottom of the page. Making the visitor work so hard to opt-in is a surefire way for them to simply not bother. On websites that prioritize email sign ups, you will find the sign up button is front and center on the home page. In fact, you will see it in multiple places on the website to get people to notice it. These are called secondary locations on the website once people are navigating your website. Make sure people can sign up easily after reading your 'About us' section, or at the end of every blog post, or perhaps even explore different intent pop-ups that give the opportunity to the visitor to sign up without being too annoying. If your website has a sidebar, put an opt-in form there as well.

While you are doing this, it is also important to note how critical it is to articulate the value that they are signing up for. A simple sign up for my newsletter does not sound very convincing to any new visitor and they will fail to convert. All of us are subscribed to far too many newsletters these days and they don't need one more unless they see the real value you're giving away on your website. Tell them what they will get from your lead magnet and what you will give them in terms of regular emails or newsletters. It also helps to look at a heat map of your current website to see where most visitors are clicking to go. Once you identify those hotspots, you can look into adding more sign up forms at those hot spots to get more conversions. For instance, if it is a long article that is getting a lot of visits, could you add some sign up forms in between the article as a content upgrade? For example, if the article is about mastering the fear of cold calling, providing a script as a content upgrade can enhance the chances of conversion.

Sadly, while most business owners know the importance of digital marketing or social media marketing, they do not know how to optimize these tools to arrive at their desired results. You can have the prettiest of websites or landing pages, but if you don't have enough forms embedded in them, you will miss 100 per cent of the visitors who visit your website. You can be super consistent with your postings on social media, but if you don't include a clear call-to-action in your posts, people will simply consume your content without ever contacting you. It's a good idea to nudge people who are considering getting in touch with you through these tools and technologies. Moreover, they can be automated to a point where you can be sleeping and they can still get in touch with you. That's why they call the website your 24 hour salesperson. Day or night, if you have put all the right pieces in place, prospects who visit your website will be more than happy to download your lead magnet and engage with your content. In the next chapter, we will dive deeper into using automation to lift some of that heavy work. This is so that by the time they book a call with you on your calendar, they have already consumed your best content and are pretty warmed up to doing business with you. That's what we all inherently desire, isn't it?

Think about It

- Are your websites or landing pages optimized to generate leads?
- Do your social media posts contain a clear call-to-action?
- Does your content include an upgrade or something more that they can access with an exchange of email address or other similar details?
- Are you tracking your analytics to understand where you might be underperforming in the lead generation or sales closing process
- Are you sweating your assets to build long term relationships via the internet?

Chapter 9

Automation: Saving Time, Money, and Effort on Repetitive Tasks

As a business owner or marketer, finding ways to conserve precious resources is vital. You want to spend your time focusing on growing your business and there are some things you shouldn't have to take on by yourself, especially repetitive and administrative tasks. You can simplify the work you do with automation, the same way we have technology to do the heavy lifting for us. With the amount of marketing software that is available in the market, you can automate many of the repetitive tasks altogether and free up your time to do something that is even more productive.

Why Automate?

Let's be real. It is impossible to spend all of your time marketing. That's why we have websites and landing pages that act as our 24/7 salesperson. Actually, in this day and age, we have the capability to automate while delivering personalized results. If you don't have marketing software in the 2020s, you're seriously lagging behind!

Marketing automation is a software platform that helps you automate your marketing and sales engagement to generate more leads, close more deals, and accurately measure marketing success. Marketing automation is not the nice-to-have strategy you can ignore. If you want to compete, you need to be using marketing automation. It's the new standard, and leveraging this will make your life a lot simpler while saving you time and money. The goal is to let you and your team focus on other aspects of your business that require a human touch. According to Ledgeview Partners, nine out of ten marketers use more than one form of marketing automation on a regular basis. Research firm Nucleus noted that marketing automation improved business productivity by 20 per cent and Invespcro found that 80 per cent of companies saw an increase in leads due to marketing automation. Marketing automation is a necessity today without which, companies take the risk of falling behind their competition.

Marketing automation is technology that automates marketing processes to help teams plan, coordinate, manage, and measure the new results of campaigns across multiple channels, including web, email, display, search, and social. A marketing automation platform typically allows you to simplify and streamline many arduous and time-consuming processes, automate repetitive tasks to free up marketer's time to concentrate more on planning, decision making, and creative matters. Simply put, it reduces human error, saves on time, money, effort while maximizing efficiency and revenue.

There are a variety of tools that can help you automate parts of your marketing efforts. Email marketing software is the most common choice, and many businesses already use it. There are also other advanced platforms that can automate interactions over social media, SMS, websites and so on. These larger, more comprehensive marketing automation software allow you to capture information of your consumers, reach out to them through various channels, and track their progress through the different stages of the sales process. One of the main strengths of automation software is that it offers a variety of workflow and unique ways to engage consumers you are tracking. A workflow consists of triggers and actions. Actions are automated responses to what they do. If someone downloads an ebook off a website, it is recognized as a trigger. Then, the automated software sends them an email to notify them when the next ebook in that series is available.

All of this is prepared beforehand. Similarly, if someone signs up for a webinar, later on, the automated system sends them a related white paper. If someone subscribes to a newsletter, the automated system sends an email invite to an event that your newsletter promotes. As we provide relevant content and information to follow up on the interest that someone has shown, we entice them with valuable knowledge to engage our prospects even more and lead them down the marketing funnel to make them even more interested in making a purchase.[41]

Building Trust

When email marketing was relatively new, marketers thought of it as two simple steps.

1. Focus all your efforts on getting leads on your website. Do anything and everything possible to get people to subscribe to your mailing list.
2. Once you have subscribers, hit those subscribers with a mix of educational and promotional messages.

Back when email was a relatively new thing, this worked like a charm. Through the email channel, you had people's attention and with such low competition back then, it was easy to build up a large list and simply burn your subscribers out with promotional messages. You would lose as many subscribers, but on the whole, more promotion equaled more revenue. I remember one marketing company that was so bad I swore I will never buy a single thing from them. Not only did they bombard me with their emails after I signed up for something, they had no unsubscribe button! It was horrible. I searched all their different emails. I couldn't find any link to unsubscribe. The more I searched, the more frustrated I got. It came to the point where I simply emailed them asking how I can unsubscribe from their emails. They replied saying that the only way I could unsubscribe is by

---

[41] https://www.oracle.com/cl/a/ocom/resources/marketing-automation-101-bp-guide.pdf

emailing a certain email address notifying my wish to unsubscribe. This company was so desperate to hold on to their leads that they simply made it very, very troublesome for anyone to unsubscribe. I had to jump through multiple hoops just to get my name off their list. So take it from me, always give people the option to unsubscribe. You don't want a disengaged subscriber on your list anyway. I will share more about that later on in this chapter. These days you rarely will see this approach as it has become ineffective. The average user possibly gets around hundreds of emails a day so your subscriber's attention is divided.

Email marketing is another form of building relationships online. It's like sending letters to your loved ones or pen-pals, except you are doing it with an intention to get them to take a particular action. Whatever platform you use, you have to earn the attention of the people who subscribed to you. It is powerful in creating ongoing communication with your audience and to get people to return to your website. Email is also a strong driver of revenue for most businesses. Never take it for granted that a subscriber cares about you, your business or your emails. It takes multiple interactions between a person and a brand before that person is ready to make a purchase. Email is one of the best ways to facilitate these multiple interactions. Instead of hitting your subscribers with sales messages one after the other, give them a good reason to visit your website or make a purchase from you.

Now that you've learnt the importance of generating leads through your website or through your social media, you are now sitting on a mountain of databases of contacts. But you don't want to be sitting on this database and let it sit there unused. That would be the worst thing you could do for your marketing return on investment. The beauty of automation software is that it helps you easily build nurturing streams and progressively engage your leads. You can now offer them your best-ever piece of content and prove to them that you know what you are talking about. Once you've established the trust, you can engage with them with more sales-focused emails or ads talking about the solution that you are providing to their problems, ideally validated with case studies or rave reviews. Along the way, you can offer them a link to make a purchase or perhaps a free trial with a possibility of getting in touch with you. The key is to not rush it as people don't like being sold as much as they love to buy. They will more likely than not take their time to read, learn, and then decide. So give them time while you also take your own time to build killer high quality content.

To establish a level of trust where consumers are confident to invest in your products or services, you need to be able to nurture them. Email has long been—and still is—perhaps the highest ROI marketing tool out there. It's a bold claim, but the facts speak for themselves. For starters, here's a fun fact: everyone uses email! I've seen individuals who refuse to buy a smartphone for their mental wellness but I've not come across anyone who doesn't have an email address. You need these to get even the free things available on the internet. According to Radicati's Email Statistics Report, there are about 4.4 billion email accounts worldwide with 25 per cent being corporate accounts. McKinsey has found that we spend two and a half hours a day on business emails if we are employed or run a business. That comes to about 50 hours a month.

Moreover, when people check email, their brains are engaged as they are not in 'browsing' mode like they usually are when on social media. When the Direct Marketing Association studied the effectiveness of various types of marketing, email came out way on top with a return of investment of around forty-one to one. Nearly twice that of any other approach. This means sending emails proved to be more effective than other approaches, which translates to better sales and lowered marketing costs for businesses.

When data analytics firm Custora published the results of their four-year study into the online buying patterns of over 72 million customers across fourteen industries, they showed that over forty times as many purchases came from links in emails compared to Facebook or Instagram. Email is powerful, because it can be very personal. Emails sit in your inbox next to messages from your colleagues, friends, relatives, or clients. There is just something special about receiving an email in your personal inbox that makes it feel like it's been made just for you. This means that email marketing is a much more certain route to reaching your ideal clients than to broadcast on the web. Even if everyone doesn't open your emails, you stand a decent chance of having a number of your subscribers reading your emails. It doesn't need a super-fast broadband, a hi-fi webcam, fancy microphone or complex software.[42]

Perhaps the most popular reason people use email is because it is perfect for follow up. For generations, successful marketers and business development executives have known that the key to winning customers is through follow up. This is especially true when the product is a high value one. As mentioned in the previous chapters, you need a total of seven hours, eleven touch-points over four different mediums before they are likely to buy. Email allows you to do this by adding value, building credibility and forming trust. It allows you to track and measure who opens your emails, who is clicking your links, and who is buying from you. That means you can adapt your approach based on the facts. The ability to communicate proactively, personally, and regularly makes email marketing a powerful tool for building relationships, proving credibility and of course, driving sales.

According to Brian Carroll, the author of Lead Generation for the Complex Sale, 'up to 95 per cent of the qualified prospects on your website are there to research and are not yet ready to talk with a sales rep, but as many as 70 per cent of them will eventually buy a product from you—or your competitors'. Email marketing allows you to follow up and personalize your follow ups as well. The best part? It is scalable.

Email on Autopilot

A lot of the email marketing that is done is done as a 'broadcast'. In other words, you create an email and send it out to everyone that has subscribed to you. You could also send it out only to a subset of your entire database. Usually, these kinds of broadcasts are like announcements, announcing a new event, a new product, or sharing the latest in the format of a newsletter. These can be written beforehand and scheduled, but that's about it. You can't automate any more after that. The really interesting possibility of automation is when you utilize the

---

[42] Jacopo Mauri, 'Marketing Automation 101', *E Learning Industry*, (1 July 2019). https://elearningindustry.com/advertise/elearning-marketing-resources/blog/what-is-marketing-automation-101

'autoresponder' ability to pre-program your emails and have them sent out in sequence. When you send out a broadcast, everybody is getting the same email at the same time. However, with an autoresponder in place, you can get Email 1 when you sign up, Email 2 the next day, Email 3 a few days later. All of these can be set up in advance. Once you set it, you can pretty much forget about it and it will work like a charm. This means less time spent on compiling email lists and scheduling messages. When you send out emails manually, the size of your staff or the amount of time you have limits the number of consumers that you can reach. Would you be able to stay on schedule if your customer base suddenly doubled or tripled in size?

There are multiple benefits to email automation. Firstly, it ensures everyone will get your best emails. Imagine Andrea joined your email list yesterday, but you sent out a broadcast email three weeks ago that brought in a lot of sales. Andrea wouldn't have gotten that broadcast because it wasn't part of the automated sequence and she wasn't part of the list back then. With an automated sequence, all new subscribers can get your best stuff. Secondly, you can tailor your email sequence based on whether they are an informed consumer, afflicted consumer or in the rare case, an oblivious consumer. This is possible because the systems allow you to tag your consumers based on the options they click. For example, if you are a book coach who offers coaching and publishing services to your clientele, let's assume they opted in to your newsletter. Now, you can ask them simple questions to identify where they are on their journey. Which of the following sentences appeal the most to you?

1. The best way to raise your profile with the highest ROI (tagged as #oblivious consumer)
2. The three ways you can publish your book: traditional publishing, self-publishing, or hybrid publishing (tagged as #afflicted consumer)
3. Important factors to watch out for when you are working with a traditional publisher (tagged as #informed consumer)

Based on what they click, you can generate a different series of emails catered to where they are at in the book writing journey. All three titles appeal to consumers who are at different stages of their book journey and have different levels of awareness around the realities of writing a book. Therefore, sharing the same content to all of them will not work in your favour. However, sharing content that will move them to the next step along the journey will help to build the relationship with you. That's why it is critical for businesses to have personalized content for their consumer at the 3 different stages. You can organize this in such a way that all new subscribers click the option that appeals the most to them from above and they get tagged accordingly. This activates the series of emails that will be most beneficial for them. Each of your consumer's actions is an added data point for your marketing strategy, telling you what consumers are looking for, immediately in the moment. As helpful as this information is, tracking these behaviours manually is a chore. With marketing automation software, businesses can use these inputs across multiple channels to deeply understand their customer's needs and deliver the right content at the right time.

Create Email Sequences

Email sequences, also known as autoresponders, are sets of pre-written emails you can program into your email marketing tool and then set to send at specified times and frequencies to your subscribers. The sequences you set can boost your blog readership, increase your course sign ups, and boost sales for your ecommerce products.

These email sequences help drive qualified consumers to helpful content, resulting in warm leads that can be nurtured thoughtfully into customers. With the customer at the center of the flywheel, businesses can continue to engage customers with personalized workflows that lead to loyal, repeat purchases and brand ambassadors who refer their friends and family.

Here are four sequences that you can deploy to build your businesses faster.

1. Welcome Sequence

The first email responder every business should put in place is the welcome sequence. It is a series of five to ten emails that your new subscribers will start receiving in the days and weeks after they subscribe. The welcome sequence is super valuable because it allows your new subscribers to get to know you, learn about your products and services, and see your best and most engaging content first. When creating your welcome sequence, focus the emails around your story, the founder's story i.e. why he/she created the business, and what products and services you are offering. Make sure your welcome emails feature your best content, like high-ranking blog posts or most-watched YouTube videos.

2. The Evergreen Sales Sequence

The evergreen sales sequence is an important autoresponder to create if you are interested in converting more of your subscribers into paying customers. It consists of five emails, spread out over five to ten days, that get your subscribers to buy a specific product or service from you. This email sequence is foundational for your business because just adding people to your list and never sending them any product or service offers is a missed opportunity. Make sure to tell your subscribers what the product or service is that you are selling, where and how to buy it, what a customer gets after purchase, and the answers to common questions and objections through FAQs and testimonials.

3. Feedback Sequence

A feedback sequence gives you the opportunity to gain valuable information about your subscribers. It also helps you discover what holds certain subscribers back from becoming customers or signing up for your products or services. If you have an email autoresponder sequence that pitches one of your products in the final email, you can program a feedback email sequence to be sent a week later to any subscriber who didn't buy. These can be as simple as asking them '*Why didn't you buy?*' Create a single email asking for feedback around a specific question and be sure to answer your audience's feedback email as it builds trust and confidence in your brand. Thereafter, take action based on the feedback you get and you've got yourself a working continuous improvement feedback cycle. This sequence allows you to address the issues that are keeping subscribers from becoming customers and boost your conversions.

4. A Newsletter Sequence

A newsletter sequence allows you to promote your content consistently in the form of an email being sent at the same time and day every week. The frequency can differ as long as it is consistent. This type of email sequence also gets your subscribers used to seeing your brand pop up in their inbox at the same time each week. With a newsletter, you give your audience an overview of recent developments in your business, your new content and special offers. A consistent newsletter sequence keeps your business top-of-mind with subscribers. That makes it easy for them to seek out your products or services when faced with a problem your business solves. Even if new subscribers don't immediately purchase one of your products, there's a good chance they will in the future if you consistently communicate your value through regular emails.

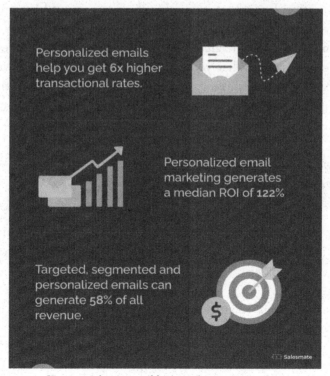

[Source: salesmate.io/blog/email-automation/]

You only need to do this once, and it's done. Set and forget. If creating that is too much work, you can also schedule emails covering the basics to be sent early in the sequence and more advanced material later on in the sequence. When you create a long enough sequence, you can slowly build them up to trigger a sale. For example, if you send them a link to make a purchase, and they click it, they automatically get tagged as a customer. Having a customer tag will automatically trigger another sequence of customer care emails. This is where your sequence will congratulate the buyer, send them information on how best to use the product or service, or reassure them of your availability and support. Having an autoresponder sequence like this can greatly reduce buyer's remorse, refunds or post-purchase anxiety. You can also have short sequences, where they get about five to ten emails on the sequence and then they get grouped into the weekly newsletter series which you send out as a broadcast.[43]

Based on the above example of the book coach, here's an outline of a short email sequence that he can use

Objective: Encourage new subscribers to sign up for a one-to-one 'write your first book' call.

Timing: It gets activated immediately when subscribers opt in for a free checklist of 'What you need to prepare before you write your book based on these three stages: Planning, Writing, Promoting'. The autoresponder sequence gets activated and you send an email every two to three days

Email 1: Did you get your checklist?
Goals:

- Ensure subscribers got the checklist and read it
- Establish friendly conversational tone and encourage interaction
- Get people to whitelist your emails so that they don't go into spam folder

Call to Action: Identify which stage of the process they are in by clicking the relevant link that tags them.

---

[43] https://blog.worldsynergy.com/marketing-automation-101/

Email 2: What are you struggling with the most?
Goals:

- Get subscribers to give you data
- Identify subscribers who are in the informed stage and ready to buy

Call to Action: Get them to reply to your email and share the challenges they face or fill up a survey form with questions on what content they would like from the Book Coach

Email 3: Top 10 problems all authors face when working with a traditional publisher
Goals:

- Influence subscribers to opt into hybrid-publishing instead of traditional publishing
- Weigh pros and cons in the book coach's favour
- Paint a positive picture of adopting a hybrid publishing model

Call to Action: Get them to book a call with the Book Coach

Email 4: How to get speaking engagements with your book
Goals:

- Excite subscribers to the possibilities of becoming a speaker by writing a book
- Share some hot tips to get speaking engagements
- Share case studies of clients who managed to get paid speaking engagements

Call to Action: Get them to book a call with the Book Coach

Email 5: The Biggest Mistake Authors after writing their book
Goals:

- Be recognized as the authority in this space

- Save them time, energy, stress and money by warning them of common mistakes
- Share case studies of mistakes other authors have made before

Call to Action: Get them to book a call with the Book Coach

In the event they manage to make a purchase, the system can automatically trigger a payment confirmation email when the user completes the transaction. Autoresponders have the ability to enhance the effectiveness of your emails and increase your sales. Putting your marketing on autopilot using autoresponders ensures that you have the time to focus on other key activities that move the needle for your business. Autoresponders can be 'storyboarded' the same way filmmakers do to achieve an overall goal.

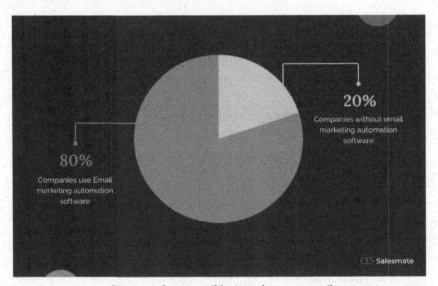

[Source: salesmate.io/blog/email-automation/]

As you build your email database, finding the right balance in your emails to get the best results will become a challenge. The bigger the variety of the subscribers in your database, the bigger the gap in expectations around topics you cover, frequency of your emails, and how much you promote your products or services. You will find some group of subscribers who feel you are not emailing them enough and another that feels you're emailing them too much. There will be some who want more emails on a specific topic and others who want more emails on different topics. There will be some who are ready to buy your product or service and others who are just not open to the idea as yet. Plus, if you try to hit the middle ground, you end up pleasing no one. This is why it is important to segment your email list. It is a technique for splitting your subscribers into groups and emailing different things to each group. By doing this you are ensuring that you're sending the right message with the right frequency to each group. When you segment a list you group subscribers into different segments with key characteristics. There are a few different ways to segment your database of subscribers.

Informed Consumer, Afflicted Consumer, and Oblivious Consumer

First, you can segment your database by interests. If you knew someone who was interested in a particular product or service, you could send your sales emails to them and spare those who aren't interested. This can either be done through tagging them based on previous emails they have opened and clicked on. Or you can email all your subscribers about a specific topic and offer more information only to those who are interested in what you have to sell. As per our Book Coach example previously, every time you send a link of your article or video, you tag the subscribers who click the link. When you launch your product you send more emails about it to the tagged subscribers, knowing that they have shown an interest in the topic, product or service. You have a higher chance of closing more sales this way as opposed to getting more people unsubscribing from your mailing list because they felt you were too 'salesy' or 'pushy'.

Another way to look at it is to provide a free, new resource and announce it to your email database. Those subscribers who take up the offer would get put on a short email sequence that then sends them the information you promised and follows up with information about your product or service—such as frequently asked questions.

If this, then that

Another cool thing that you can do with email automation is to tailor the emails you send to subscribers based on their level of engagement. So if there are five emails in your sequence, instead of sending them one day apart as per a schedule, you can configure it based on engagement. That means email #2 will only get sent if the link to email #1 was clicked. If there was no click, they don't get the next email in the sequence. This way, the subscribers that reach the finish line i.e. end of the sequence, are the ones who are most engaged. For those who haven't consumed the first piece of content in the sequence, they won't get access to the second, third, fourth and fifth piece as well. Another way you can leverage the segmentation feature is to try and re-engage with subscribers who have stopped opening and reading your emails. The great thing about these email softwares is that it provides you with the data. It tells you who opened your emails, which email subject lines had a higher open rate, who clicked on the links in your emails and so on. This means you can add disengaged subscribers into a separate automation sequence purely to re-engage with them. If they still fail to re-engage, they are weeded out of your email list, which makes the email list a lot more high quality. You either get a re-engaged subscriber or an inactive subscriber removed from your list. This increases the deliverability of your emails in the long run.

You might have a list of consumers that don't buy your services anymore due to some reason. Their requirements may have changed in recent times and this is where you need to reconnect with them. You can get them to engage again with your business by adding them to your mailing list and bringing them back on board. Re-engagement can be highly effective when you do it the right way. According to salesmate, offering free resources has the highest percentage—39 per cent effectiveness—in re-engaging your database, compared to selling a new product, providing customer testimonials, coupons, and surveys.

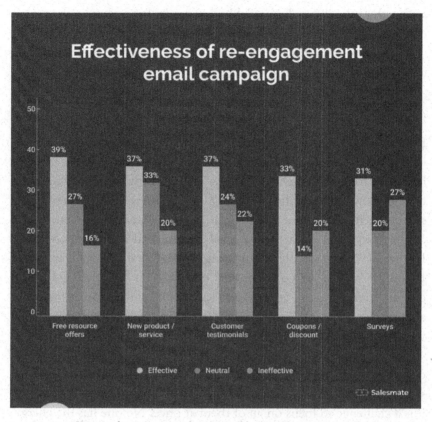

[Source: https://www.salesmate.io/blog/email-automation/]

Email automation allows you to create workflows for every action that the consumer takes and sends emails based on those triggers. You can personalize these emails for each trigger and automate them. In short, you can create a flowchart with a series of yes/no actions. If the consumer clicks the buy link, send a series of emails to increase the chances for the sale. If the consumer doesn't click any link, then you can automate another workflow that goes into educating the consumer about your products and services without giving any offers. Automated email brings 320 per cent more revenue than emails that are part of a non-automated campaign. In the case of the book coach, if someone clicks to book an appointment two weeks later, where you set up the calendar to be available two weeks from current date, you can also activate a workflow to send emails to remind them about the appointment as well as value add to them by giving them valuable content to consume before the call.

Are you ready to automate?

Despite all the benefits of automation, it is important to have a clear idea of when you should embark on implementing automation in your business. You have to ask yourself if you are already generating a steady flow of new and qualified leads. Do you have a content marketing strategy mapped to your buyer's journey? Are you tracking your leads' digital body language across each touchpoint and marketing channel? Do you have a proven lead nurturing strategy that you want to scale? If you are publishing good content, generating a steady flow of new, organic leads, and you are ready to scale your efforts, chances are you are ready to focus your efforts on a marketing automation strategy that will nurture quality leads into paying customers.

Good marketing has the ability to set you apart from your competition. However, it can be hard to keep track of what marketing strategies work and which ones don't. Even when you do keep track, it is a challenge to focus on all of them at once. No one has the energy to do it. That's why marketing automation exists to make marketing easier for you, and your team. Marketing automation is a mixture of strategy, software, and customer-centricity. It allows you to nurture prospects with highly personalized, useful content that helps convert prospects to delighted customers, and customers to loyal advocates. Weaving automation throughout your business will break down silos and unite teams with processes that save time. Combined with the human touch, marketing automation can do wonders for your business and keep it growing.

What if they don't open my emails?

Now you can imagine the frustration of going through the tedious processes to set up the marketing automation systems only to realize from the email platform insights that your emails are not being opened. Trust me, I've been there, and I know how it feels. If you want your subscribers to open up your emails, then three things need to happen.

1. Your emails have to end up in the inbox and not in the spam folder which your consumers don't check often

Your first challenge is to make sure your emails get through to your subscribers. For that, your emails must not get classified as spam. The spam filters for email look at the reputation of the email address and the email system that sends out the emails. If the email address has been reported as one that is spamming, it can automatically block further emails from that address. Alternatively, if the email system is one that most spammers are known to use, all emails from that system can also be blocked out.

The spam filter systems check if the address or the system has been flagged as spam before. They also check to see where the links in the email go to and if those links are connected to domains associated with previous spam reports. On top of that, these algorithms also look into how many times your email has been flagged as spam by your own subscribers. One of the biggest causes of this is a mismatch between what a subscriber signed up for and what he got instead. That's why it's critical for you to let them know what they're signing up for in the form itself. If you are going to be sending promotional emails, mention it. Be transparent about it. Aside from that, you also have to ensure you stay on topic. If your subscribers signed up for investment tips, telling them your travel stories won't resonate very well. As a rule of thumb, if they're not expecting it, don't send it.

The more your subscribers open your emails, the more time they spend reading them, reply to them, or click links on them, the more likely it is that future emails from you will stay out of the spam folder. The solution is simple to ensure your emails end up in the inbox. Make sure your emails have great content and are enjoyable to read. Another way to tackle this is to get all your subscribers to reply to your email to confirm they got the lead magnet that they downloaded. You can switch this up with a survey to learn more about them or simply ask them to whitelist your emails by adding you to their contacts list in their email system.

2. They have to open your emails

The last thing standing between your well-crafted email and your subscribers is a great subject line. In order to get your subscribers to open up your emails, you need to leverage human psychology. The subject line along with your pre-header text compete with hundreds of other emails in your subscriber's inbox. If you get the messaging right, they will open your email.

i) Personalize it

Email marketing is one of the most personal forms of marketing communication. The ability to target individuals allows you to personalize your messaging which improves your conversions. Insert your reader's name into the email subject line to increase open rate. When a reader sees his or her name in the subject line, something happens in their brain where they need to see what it is. This level of personalization is easy to implement. You can also refer to your reader's location. People feel a connection to their hometown. When you include location-specific language in the subject line, your readers will be curious about what is happening in the area. You can also highlight your reader's interests by calling out something that means a lot to them in the subject line.

ii) Make it relevant

In some cases, personalization isn't as effective. If it is not, your goal is to write effective email subject lines that are relevant to your target audience. You need to clearly communicate something that the reader either really wants or needs. You can do that by being specific in the email subject line. For example, which email subject headline is more descriptive?

a) Guaranteed returns today!

or

b) Five ways to help increase your returns by 20 per cent

Subject line A is not very detailed and makes a big claim with nothing to support it. On the other hand, line B lets the reader know exactly what to expect in the email. The best subject lines make a promise and then deliver on the promise. If you don't deliver on your promise, your bounce rate will go through the roof. Email marketing that is relevant means sending the right messages to the right people. Tailor it to your readers' interests and desires. Instead of blasting out an email to your entire email list, you can increase relevance by segmenting your audience into smaller groups. When you send emails to smaller groups of your list, you can get more specific based on that group's interests and desires. According to copywriter Gary Bencivenga, the formula for writing advertising headlines is as simple as this:

Interest = Benefit + Curiosity

The same works for emails. People who are made curious will be more motivated to open emails that promise something useful. However, if they think they already know what is going to be in the email, they will skip it. This is where you have to go back to the benefits based on your customer insights and look at their goals and aspirations. Dive deeper into their pains and problems. So if you are in the topic of fitness and one of the areas that your clients struggle with is exercise, then you can explore further on the causes of obesity. You can expand on the topic and add curiosity into the subject line in a number of ways. Here are a few examples:

1. The how to headline

How to [Desirable Outcome] (Even If [Obstacle])
How to [Desirable Outcome] (Without [Obstacle])
How to [Desirable Outcome] (While You [Desirable Outcome])

We're naturally drawn to emails that tell us how to do something in a practical way. This classic headline template almost never fails.

Rather than just a vague thought-exercise, it promises a practical way of achieving something.

Examples

- How to Grow Your Mailing List
- How to Train Your Dog
- How to Lose Weight

Adding Shock Value

Add shock value by turning the irresistible result into a more tangible, more specific benefit. Make the common obstacles something really frustrating to your audience, and similarly make the pleasant action something very desirable.

- How to Grow Your Mailing List (Even If You Have No Website)
- Surprisingly Effective Ways to Train Your Dog (Without Raising Your Voice)
- How to Rapidly Lose Weight (While Gorging Yourself on Delicious Chocolate)

2. The ultimate guide headline

- The Ultimate Guide to Affiliate Marketing
- The Ultimate Guide to Green Smoothies
- The Ultimate Guide to HDR Photography

This template doesn't need any added shock value. The 'ultimate' is shocking in itself. There's a catch though this headline will only work if your content is truly detailed and informative. If you're able to dazzle your readers with a vast guide of incredibly valuable information, the shock value and shareability is in the content.

Warning: If your content is good, but not really ultimate guide material, skip this headline. If everything you write is an ultimate guide, feel free to use it every time.

3. The list headline

X Things That [Obstacle]
X Ways to [Desirable Outcome]
These X Things Are [Unpleasant Result]
X [Topic] Mistakes

A 'list headline' takes many forms, but always comes with a number. The power of the headline is giving the reader an exact amount of content they're getting. It can be a huge list, which allures the reader with its huge amount of information, or it can be a list of five, which is an easily approachable bitesize bit of content.

- Five Things That Are Making You Unhappy
- 101 Ways to Save Money
- These Seven Things Are Unhealthy For Your Teeth
- Five List Building Mistakes

Add shock value with a more specific topic, more colourful word choices, and more drastic results.

- Five Everyday Things That Are Destroying Your Happiness
- 101 Surprising Ways to Save Money and Get Rich
- Warning! These Seven Things Are Rotting Your Teeth
- Five Fatal List Building Mistakes You Don't Know You're Making

To get a full list of headline examples, head over to www.vivekiyyani. com/free to download all the bonus worksheets and exercises.

iii) Build your reputation

The long term strategy to getting your subscribers to open up your emails is to focus on building a strong reputation for yourself. Think about it. If you were to receive an email from your spouse, your friends or your boss, you open them up no matter what time of day or night it is, regardless of the subject line. That's the level you have to aim for. If your lead magnet delivers tremendous insights then your initial emails will be received with tremendous anticipation. If they turn out to be full of value, your subscribers will make a mental note to tag your emails as one of those people whose emails they try to open whenever possible. Over time, it becomes a habit to read your emails and expect them. That's why you should look to incorporate call-to-action in your emails as a way to make it a habit to click the links you provide. That's it. If you can achieve these three outcomes, you will attain the high ROI that comes with email marketing.

Advertisements for Millennials

Now, I know I mentioned early on in this book about how Millennials tend to think about advertisements. They have become so accustomed to it that they have become immune to it. To be fair, the nature of media and advertisement has been changing constantly. With every new generation, old rules are thrown out or reconsidered when it no longer provides the same ROI. The same old advertising techniques won't work on the Millennial generation. With this group attached to their smart phones, tablets and laptops, with access to social media and the Internet, and the way they find, consume, and act on all information is completely different from previous generations. Millennials have turned traditional advertising on its head, requiring an entirely new approach. People haven't stopped buying things but the way they buy, the how, as well as the why, have changed. When trying to figure out if something is worth buying, Millennials will go to their friends and social networks to see what people think. This is a collective filter that they use as a means to sort out research and other word-of-mouth information as they make decisions. Millennials don't enjoy being talked at. They are used to controlling information with their fingertips and the way they interact with brands is no different. They know what's good for them and what's bad. If you give them the goods, they will share it with their networks on social media platforms. In an age where information is shared instantaneously, the Millennial generation is incredibly adept at filtering out the things they don't want.

That does not mean ads don't work. They do, and are a critical part of the marketing strategy. The only difference that I would highlight and emphasize on is that ads should be used as an accelerator. There is no point pouring petrol in a car with flat tires. Unfortunately, this is what we see across many businesses today. They go to social media ads as the first step to generating leads, appointments and sales. However, they fail to realize the power of identifying organic content that is already resonating with your connections on your network. Content is really king to the younger generation, and the more creative the better. When you have a habit of posting consistently on social media, you are effectively collecting data about which piece of content is resonating with your network. That's why social media mogul Gary Vaynerchuck constantly talks about churning out multiple pieces of content daily. Something is eventually bound to stick and when it does, you know this is a piece of content you can accelerate even further by running ads on it. In essence, the organic content you put out can be seen as a proof-of-concept of what will really resonate with people across the board when you run ads to it. Instead, what we see a lot of companies and agencies do is to create a completely new piece of content that hasn't been verified as content that is engaging. Pushing out your content that has collected a significant amount of organic views, likes, comments and shares becomes a safe choice of creative to put out as an ad.

The truth is no amount of paid media is going to turn a bad piece of content into good content. Just in the same way that no amount of investors' money is going to save a bad product. That is why I fully believe in investing in the long game of improving your brand's content by creating a lot of it. When something clicks, study it, understand what about it resonated with your audience, and then accelerate its views by running ads on it. If you are a small business, you want to focus on spending your time, money and effort on creating great content. Apply the Pareto principle here, which says: The Pareto principle, also known as the 80/20 rule, states that roughly 80 per cent of the effects come from 20 per cent of the causes. In marketing terms, the Pareto principle suggests that a small portion of a company's efforts or customers will account for a disproportionate amount of its revenue or success. For example, a company might find that 80 per cent of its sales come from just 20 per cent of its customers. Alternatively, a company might find that 80 per cent of its website traffic comes from just 20 per cent of its blog posts. By identifying these 'high-impact' areas, a company can focus its efforts on what is most likely to drive success. Spend 80 per cent of your marketing budget on creating quality content and 20 per cent on amplifying the high quality content. Going all in on organic social content with a small amplification budget will help you achieve more valuable results.

Therefore, ads should come last in your strategy once you have multiple pieces of content that act as a positive proof-of-concept. They worked well organically, so it is safe to assume that the marketing dollars you pour onto this piece of creative will have a significantly higher ROI. The biggest thing people don't understand is that quality content is so critical to marketing to Millennials. Anyone in that demographic discovers a business for the first time by either Google search or finding their content on social media. If you are not focusing on the content that you put out on the most important social platforms, you're going to become moot and obsolete in the modern day of doing business. That's why organic reach is so important because the impression you get when someone comes directly to your page is a much more qualified lead and potentially a more valuable customer than someone you got through an ad buy.

Hitting these five bases

What I've shared with you may seem simple, with just five areas to focus on. However, never underestimate the power of simplicity. Built into these five outcomes to attract Millennials you will find there is clarity, credibility, visibility, scalability and profitability. I'm pretty confident that over the next twelve months, I will get emails from readers emailing me their success stories, as a result of following the 5A framework detailed in this book. Emails of having put in the work, pushing through their limiting beliefs and executing on the five steps in the order as mentioned. They will share their observations of a better engagement level with Millennials as well as the opportunities that have started to come their way, more money and more fun. They will share their deepened understanding of the Millennial generation and express their true appreciation of their common characteristics. It is my sincere hope and wish to hear your story, to see your email in my inbox, telling me how you have managed to capture the Millennial market based on the 5A framework. In the next chapter, I will share with you some of the things I've noticed when watching highly successful people's decisions versus people who are perpetually going around in circles. It will offer you ideas on how you can overcome obstacles and achieve your goal of marketing to Millennials effectively without so many struggles.

Think about It

- How confident are you with technology? Is that hindering your growth? Think about outsourcing this to others if you find it too complicated.
- Are you leveraging automation technologies to save your time and effort on repeated tasks? How much can you save in terms of time?
- Have you invested resources into growing your email database?
- Do you have an email nurturing system to continuously engage your community?
- Are you running ads to your top performing organic content on social media?

Chapter 10

Your Next Marketing Adventure

If you thought marketing is all about influencing behaviour, let me tell you, Millennials will influence you before you even get to them. In fact, their impact on marketing is already being seen and felt pretty evidently. The language we use, the platforms we use to market, the creatives we work on to engage have been influenced by Millennials! People of all generations look to the Millennials to see what is trending and 'top-of-mind' on social media. Millennials have made their mark as a generation of consumers to be reckoned with. They have their own signature style of working, buying, communicating and leading. The leaders who truly get what they stand for—their identity, values, beliefs, behaviours, expectations—are best positioned to win.

Embracing Artificial Intelligence for Marketing

As technology continues to improve, people will rely more and more on artificial intelligence to get things done. As I write this book, there is a new kid on the block that's getting all the attention: ChatGPT. While ChatGPT is more than a search engine, many people are using it primarily to find information. Microsoft, which is invested in OpenAI, the company that worked on this new tool, is also looking to morph its Bing search engine to incorporate ChatGPT. This is an attempt to cut into Google's 90 per cent search market share. ChatGPT takes personalization to a new level. It can learn from previous conversations you have had with the language model and understand your context and preferences. The answers provided by this tool are tailored to your specific needs which are way more accurate than what you would find on Google. According to Accenture, 91 per cent of consumers are more likely to shop with brands that provide personalized offers and recommendations.

ChatGPT is also empowered to understand natural language queries and provide accurate and helpful responses, even if you don't use specific keywords. For general information searching, this potentially makes it easier for you to find the information you need, without having to spend time refining your search terms. The uniqueness of this tool is that it can hold a conversation with the user and provide more information in an engaging way. It makes it easier for people to understand complex topics and get the information they need in a more natural and intuitive way. According to a study conducted by Drift, companies with conversational, informal marketing with website visitors have a 10X higher conversion rate than those who don't. It's almost like Jarvis from the Marvel movie, Ironman.

Knowing how to use AI tools like ChatGPT will become increasingly important. It will be crucial for marketers to know how to ask ChatGPT the right questions so that it can deliver the desired results.

The Future Ahead

Moreover, ChatGPT is just the beginning of AI and its involvement in everything we do. For marketers, there will be a whole new suite of AI tools coming out very shortly because AI is rising like a wave at the moment. By 2030, there will be exponential improvements of computer processing power, voice recognition, image recognition, deep learning, and other software algorithms. Likewise, natural language processing technologies like GPT-3 are constantly being updated and surpassed.

By 2030, most VR screens will have 8K resolution, which is four times the number of pixels on 4K screens. Most VR headsets could include the option for a brain-computer interface to record the user's electrical signals, enabling actions to be directed by merely thinking about them. Headbands and wristbands with non-invasive sensors could become the preferred choice for mainstream brain-computer interface use. Imagine how marketing will change when the mass population owns VR headsets!

By 2030, 6G could replace 5G and some experts estimate it to be 100 times faster than 5G. At that speed, it's possible to download 142 hours of Netflix movies in one second. The Internet of Things will have the potential to grow by further orders of magnitude.

In short, technology is on an upward spiral and if it's already making your head spin, it's time to prepare for more. Despite all the hype of these technologies, as a marketer, the one thing you need to remember is you don't need to worry about the technology as long as you are constantly getting a pulse of your target audience. As the years go by, technology will continue to shape the behaviours of the next generation that comes after Millennials and Gen Zs. What we as marketers need to do is to ensure we study our target audience really well so that we can continue to serve them better no matter how complex the world gets in the future ahead.

A Few things to Remember

As you embark on your next marketing adventure, here are a few things to remember to make your journey a lot smoother. The pandemic startled every businessperson and marketer across the globe. It has created a kind of havoc that people will live to tell stories about. People were forced to alter their lifestyles during the lockdown period and those changes have had a profound effect on people's behaviours. Consumer behaviour changed quite drastically. Online shopping became the norm for those who had never shopped online before. Marketers explored different ways to get in front of their target market. Property agents used virtual-reality based options to help their prospective clients get a virtual tour of the property. Fishmongers used Facebook live sessions to sell fish from the market. Hotels transformed their lounges into 'work-from-hotel' offers to provide people with the environment they needed to work in peace. Whatever the crisis, marketers need to be able to handle the challenge that is thrown at them in times like these. As marketers, we day-trade attention, and you should be really focused on identifying what Millennials are paying attention to during the transitions of their day, especially the three that occur in the home. What do Millennials do during the first fifteen minutes of their day or the first fifteen minutes after they knock off from work, and the last fifteen minutes before they go to sleep at night. These are transition periods. It's during these moments that we take stock of the next few days of our lives. We are busy, so we want to do it fast. Last time, we simply pulled out a piece of paper and a pen and wrote a to-do list. Today, it's hard to tell what people do because we have so many personalized services that appeal to us. Some may still use pen and paper. Others might have a specific app they use. The key is to pay keen attention to the details and observe with patience.

More often than not, Millennials who are in transit or taking breaks from their regular activities spend their time during the downtime scrolling through social media until something hooks them. It is critical that you are able to articulate to your stakeholders on how your content builds relationships through different touch points and platforms. Today, there are many micro-touch points where you can market and sell to consumers quickly. However, to actually convert the attention you capture in the short windows into actual sales, you need to build strong relationships with your customers and stakeholders and have consistency in your narratives across various platforms. You can't just capture the attention of someone on social media and abandon the relationship or show something incongruent with the rest of your content. Essentially, every touchpoint must be connected, which is achieved by understanding the role the particular medium plays in your overall narrative.

As a new-age marketer, you have to be prepared to deal with objections from stakeholders who don't understand the full picture. Here are some common objections that you might face when you propose marketing strategies to Millennials that might seem radical at first.

But We Have Always Done it This Way!

This is basically an argument to the status quo. While I do think we need to be grateful to the things that got us to where we are today, what got you here won't get you there. Cold calling or print ads might have been working just fine for you, so keep doing that. At the same time, it would be wise of you to create more pipelines to supplement the source of leads for your business. As long as it doesn't take away from your current level of business activity, it is a good idea to explore newer ways to market the business. It can be difficult to stop whatever you've been doing to adopt something completely new. It's much easier to pivot by adding on more sources of lead generations instead of replacing them. Refusing to change will only help you end up like Nokia and Kodak. Encourage a mindset of experimentation. I call it the 90-day runway. If you don't see any results in the first thirty days, work on perfecting your strategy. Fill the gaps and holes. Record your results and review your efforts. If it still doesn't work in the next thirty days, get feedback from another person within the team or department. Sometimes they can pick up something obvious that was in our blindspot. Now if you still don't see any results after the last thirty days, it's time to move on to the next strategy. It's easy to stick to what we know and continue with that. Our nervous system loves it because it keeps us safe. But you're smarter than that. You have to keep experimenting. Fail forward.

Why Focus on Creating Content When it Brings in Results Slowly?

The fast versus slow argument is a totally valid argument. No one wants to wait for six months to see any kind of real results. A lot of marketers love advertising because it is fast. When you don't have time to build up your rankings, you simply buy the top position. However, what many marketers fail to realize is that running ads is like a tap. As long as the ads are running, chances are high that you will be able to bring in the money. But what happens when you don't have enough cash flow to run ads? Your leads immediately stop which means your sales immediately stop. Keep in mind that every investment in advertising disappears the minute you stop. The visibility created from advertising disappears the moment you stop paying for that ad. Content, on the other hand, can be useful in conversation. It lives on the website and can be pinned on most social media platforms for people to see it as a permanent fixture. Content is more of a long-term investment, where you invest your time and creativity to bring out organic traffic. Ads may be fast but they are costly and temporary. Content may be slow, but it has a longer shelf life in generating leads. Moreover, if you are working on a piece of content, you can actually reach out to your audience and ask them for a contributor quote. The very act of creating content and reaching out to your audience has played a part in bringing your prospect closer towards a sale. Similarly, you can reach out to companies that don't even know about you yet, and ask them for an interview for your new webinar series. You get networking benefits and potential sales pipeline benefits before your piece of content even goes live. Using content to start conversations is every bit as fast as advertising and highly micro-targeted. Moreover, as mentioned in the previous chapters, content can be repurposed into multiple formats to generate an omnipresence that raises your visibility.

What is the ROI on This?

This is a very valid question, which you need to have answers to. The only way to answer this question is by making sure you do your research and collect the data. Have you collected enough data to ensure this works? Has it worked for your company? Has it worked for your competitors? Creating case studies like these will help you influence stakeholders who need to be persuaded before they give you their buy-in. Of course, the better the results, the easier this will be. But what do you do if you don't have any data? Look outside of your industry. Do you see other players implementing this strategy? How can you do the same and innovate for your own industry? All you need to do is make a strong case for marketing in a different way. If you still can't find any data, look at the top marketing agencies and see if they are doing the same. If the top marketing agencies are following a strategy that you want to implement in your own organization, it lends a certain amount of credibility to your suggestion to do something out of the norm. The most important part is to make sure you do your homework and constantly have a reputation of taking calculated risks that have paid off well.

It's Too Difficult and Cumbersome!

Like everything else, anything new is difficult before it is easy. That's just how it is. But you can't say that to your stakeholders. Remember when cold calls were the main method of prospecting? Dreadful isn't it? Yet we still see it as one of the best ways to get in touch with prospects. Everyone will have that one thing that they don't want to do in marketing. Some hate to write cold emails because they aren't good at writing. Some hate to do Facebook ads because it's too technical and makes your head spin. Some hate on social media and say it doesn't work because they haven't seen any results and find it a complete waste of time. There's something that sucks for every strategy. What you need to do is to highlight how much more difficult it would be for them to not take action. Everyone has a comfort zone, and they struggle to step out of it until it becomes an absolute must for them. Logically it may make sense to change. It may feel like an attractive option emotionally to change as well. However, when there is no urgency to make that change, people tend to procrastinate. So do the thing that encourages change: make it a lot simpler to execute and emphasize on the urgency of getting started. Breaking down the new initiatives into smaller bits helps stakeholders visualize the outcomes better. Create shorter milestones to hit and allocate the work to be done in different stages. This makes it look much more manageable and prevents overwhelm.

Can't We Just Outsource This?

Of course, outsourcing is one of the ways you can manage a portion of your marketing if you are already overwhelmed. However, it is important to note that outsourcing marketing can be an expensive endeavour compared to doing it in-house. It all depends on your situation. I remember a quote on outsourcing marketing that stuck with me.

'When You Outsource Your Marketing, You Outsource Your Results'

Simply put, if you don't know how to market, you will always be dependent on someone who does. This puts you or your organization in a very vulnerable position. The smarter alternative is to train up and acquire the skills. The beauty of learning something on your own is that it can never be stolen from you. People can steal your talent, your ideas, your methodologies but no one can steal your skill sets.

As a marketer or business owner, building your marketing skill sets is one of the best ways to ensure you are future-proofing your business. Outsourcing marketing is a viable option once you know what needs to be done and how an extended team can speed things up for you under your direction. Otherwise, you might not know if you're getting the best value for the investment you put to outsource it. Here's what you can do instead. Play to your strengths and outsource your weaknesses. Not good at Facebook ads and have no interest whatsoever in learning it? Outsource it. If you're better at churning out content in the form of articles or videos, then double down on that. Many times, people punish themselves by forcing themselves to do something that just doesn't come easily to them. Refer back to Chapter 4 to identify your strengths and sharpen that saw.

Version 1 Will Always Come before Version 2

As much as we want to rise to a certain level of quality when we embark on the journey, the truth is that it takes multiple iterations. Your version 1 will always become before version 2, which means your work won't immediately stand out. It will take multiple iterations to get it right.

Don't Wait to Get All Your Ducks in a Row

Deep down, you know it's just a complex way of procrastinating. I know it because I'm guilty of it too. Have you observed this? Perhaps with yourself or someone you know. Whenever we start on something new, we tend to want to execute on everything perfectly. With a tendency to want to execute everything perfectly, it becomes super easy to over analyze everything we need to execute with perfection. This is what I mean by getting all your ducks in a row. It usually shows up like this:

- 'I'll get started on recording videos once I buy the right equipment'
- 'I'll start Facebook ads once I start posting more actively on Facebook'

- 'I'll write more articles once I take a professional photo for LinkedIn'
- 'I'll start networking once I buy that new suit'

We all have some of these things that we need to get done before we actually embark on the strategy that can get us the results we desire. Sometimes it is because we are afraid to make mistakes and it's natural to feel afraid to make mistakes when it's something you have not yet done before. It's normal to feel like you need to get it 'right' because you want to be successful. However, overthinking things can lead to analysis paralysis. It sounds counterintuitive but getting started and taking messy, imperfect action can lead you to success faster than waiting to get all your ducks in a row. This might sound like common sense, which brings me to my next point.

Common Sense isn't Common Practice

Knowing and doing is not the same thing. Once we learn something, which often means reading or listening to it, we assume that we will apply it in the world. Yet in the moment we respond to situations emotionally or based on habit, our common sense gets left behind. Instincts often conflict with wisdom because our social desire to feel safe overrides common sense. It takes months of effort to train yourself to master new habits for your behaviour. This is work that no amount of knowledge can replace. That's because there are four stages of competence that one needs to go through in order to achieve mastery.

1. Ignorance

In this stage, the individual does not understand or know how to do something and does not recognize the deficit. They may deny the usefulness of the skillset. They must recognize their own incompetence and the value of the skill before they move on to the next stage. For instance, learning how to fly a drone for a videographer may not seem as a crucial skill when shooting videos. However, upon seeing how much more he can charge upon picking up this skill and shooting videos with a drone, he might consider picking it up.

2. Awareness

In this stage, the individual does not understand how to do something. They recognize this as a deficit, as well as the value of a new skill in addressing the deficit. It is during this stage that the individual must focus on learning, which includes making mistakes and learning from those as well. Having a sense of 'perfectionism' will only deter the individual from learning. Flying a drone requires learning. You can't fly it the same way you drive a remote controlled car. Picking up those pieces of information is critical for the individual to fly the drone properly. Otherwise, he might lose control of the drone and it can crash and break into a thousand pieces. That being said, having a fear of breaking the drone can also limit the individual from picking up the skill.

3. Learning

In this stage, the individual understands or knows how to do something. However, demonstrating the skill or knowledge requires concentration. It may be broken down into steps, and there is heavy conscious involvement in executing the new skill. Flying a drone at this stage seems do-able, but the videographer must pay close attention to the details. If he checks his phone while his drone is in mid-flight, he might lose control of it and cause it to crash.

4. Mastery

In this final stage, the individual has had so much practice with a skill that it has become 'second nature' and can be performed easily. As a result, the skill may be performed while executing another task. The individual may be able to teach it to others, depending upon how and when it was learned. For instance, the videographer can fly the drone while talking to his friends at the same time. He has reached a level of confidence to be able to allocate his attention effectively between different tasks. Interesting, isn't it? Simply reading about marketing only gets you to the awareness level. If you want to really see results, you have to put in the work. You have to let go of your fear of failure. You have to manage the expectations of stakeholders. You have to brace for impact if you make mistakes, and learn from it. Most importantly, you must implement. And the speed of implementation plays a huge role in achieving mastery.

Speed of Implementation

Everyone wants more in life. Yet, not everyone will act on ideas that can lead to getting more. It is not enough that you learn the skill. It is equally important for you to ensure you put it into practice as soon as possible. In most cases, the level of mastery you attain with a new skill is highly dependent on your speed of implementation. The faster you implement, the faster you make mistakes and learn from it, and go through the four levels of competence. Moreover, with faster implementation, you can validate ideas faster, save time finding out what works or doesn't work in your industry, save money if something isn't worth pursuing, achieve your objectives quicker and get more things done. Our capacity to adopt the speed of implementation will determine how fast we get ahead and achieve what we want. This is a habit that you can develop. It takes practice to develop this habit. If you are able to accelerate the velocity between the time you get the idea and the time you start taking action, that very often is going to make the biggest difference. To improve your speed of implementation, document the ideas you need to take action on. Identify important items, break down big goals into smaller ones and rank them in order of importance to achieving your goals. Focus on checking off the items before going on to the next one. Then, hold yourself accountable by sharing your ideas and intentions with your team or accountability partner. Give them the permission to hold you to task to implement quickly.

New Data, New Decisions

Along the way, you will have new findings and revelations. Sometimes, you get data that suggests you are moving in the wrong direction. This is where it gets tricky. You've invested a lot of resources to get to this point. Your reputation may even be on the line. Moving forward may be a step backwards to achieving your goal. Do you still proceed? Or do you pivot? This is where you have to be able to practice agility. If the data is painting a clear picture that moving forward is not the right path, then you have actually saved yourself and your team a whole lot of pain and problems. Imagine going all the way to the end only to realize that everything you invested in was a waste of resources? Not exactly the best way to find out, isn't it? If you notice the red flags along the way, feel free to change direction. With new data, you make new decisions. No one is grounding you to finish the journey. At the end of the day, if it doesn't support you to achieve the goals that were set, it is better to change route as soon as possible. Changing your mind is not a sign of losing integrity. It is often a mark of gaining wisdom. Realizing you were wrong doesn't mean you lack judgment. It means you lacked knowledge. Opinions are about what you think today. Growth comes from staying open to revising your views tomorrow. Remember, new data, new decisions.

Success is Sequential, Not Simultaneous

As you look at the path ahead, decide on one strategy that you believe will bring in the best results. A wealthy person doesn't become wealthy overnight. A champion doesn't start winning on day one. Your skills in marketing are built over time and they in turn make your marketing campaigns successful. Success builds on success, sequentially. What appears as an overnight success is actually the result of compounded effort over a long time. This is especially true when it comes to marketing. You only have limited time and resources. It is not possible to do everything at the same time. When you prioritize in a way where you're focusing on the right thing at the moment, everything after that subsequently falls into place like a progression of dominoes. According to physicist Lorne Whitehead, a single domino can bring down another domino that is 50 per cent bigger.[44] When you pursue your goals by starting with the one, right thing, it leads to bigger things. The energy builds up in a geometric progression. You line up your priorities and focus on the first domino until you topple it. You begin with a linear process that becomes geometric.

Identify the marketing strategy you want to go with and the milestones you need to hit as you embark on this journey. Then focus on knocking out each milestone out of the park. Work on a roadmap and highlight each milestone you need to achieve on it.

Your Marketing Roadmap

Based on the chapters you have read in this book, plan out your marketing strategy for the next 100 days. Identify the audience you want to reach out to. Look at the digital assets you have and the new assets that you will need to build. Make a game plan to work alongside the algorithms for maximum reach and relatability. Acquire your own traffic by focusing on capturing the visitors who visit your website or social media profiles. Add value. Educate and entertain them. Push out your content and experiment daily. Once you find a few winners, run ads against them and look into automating it. Make your marketing as seamless as possible. When you come up with your roadmap, when you put pen to paper, it makes things a lot easier to execute upon. You got this.

One Last Thing

Congratulations! You've gotten so far with this book to the final chapter. Thank you for staying with me through these ten chapters. You may not agree or subscribe to my point of view on everything, but if this book can serve as a jolt, a wake-up call, or inspire you in any

---

[44] Ricardo Proetto, 'The One Thing', *Linkedin*, (19 December 2020). https://www.linkedin.com/pulse/one-thing-riccardo-proetto/

way, my purpose in writing this book is served. As you've probably learned by now, this book is not for people who want a quick fix in marketing to Millennials. To succeed in the long haul, you must have an authentic reason why you're in business, something that sets you apart from everyone else. Your point of difference isn't what you do but how you do it. It's always easier to start reading a book than it is to finish it, especially in today's world where we are so distracted by everything that's going on around us. Give yourself a pat on the back for getting to this point. Throughout the book, we have talked about the different rules when it comes to marketing to Millennials. This book is not for people who want a quick fix to building a brand. The steps I've outlined in this book are not a quick process. They're not the only way to succeed. However, you approach your own business, it is essential to focus on engaging Millennials by meeting them where they are at. It is about giving them value and being authentic while you do it. I am confident that by implementing the new rules of marketing to this group, the experience of marketing will be an enjoyable one that drives business results.

Everything you have learned in this book is simple, is easy to implement, and better still, it works. However, everything I've shared in this book may not work with all of the people all the time. It just works with most of the people most of the time. So there is a chance that some of the ideas you implement are working some of the time. If it doesn't work at other times, please do not stop. Keep at it. I know how hard it is to get a business started. I know how hard it is to hit your target KPIs as a marketer. I also know how easy it is to feel alone when you're on this journey. It wasn't as easy to connect with thought leaders a decade ago than it is now, and I've made it a point to make sure I respond to every reader who reaches out. Send me a message and tell me what you thought. After all, by buying this book (or borrowing it from a library), you've invested your time with me, and if there's a way, I would love to return the favour. You can always reach me at vivek@ millennialminds.sg or connect with me on LinkedIn at www.linkedin. com/in/millennialexpertasia.

What's Next

The one thing I wish printed books could do was to update itself. You know, like an app that updates itself with the latest bug fixes on our smartphones? Like it or not, that technology hasn't poured over to physical books. As a reader who loves the smell of books, I can tell you nothing beats the feeling of holding a book and reading it with a hot cup of chocolate, when it's raining outside on a typical weekend. Yet, the reality is that physical books can only be updated through their revised editions, which is a resource-intensive activity. For a subject like marketing, where things change rapidly, it's crucial for the reader to get the latest updates on the subject. If you would like to continue this journey with me, to learn the latest on 'Marketing to Millennials', then I recommend that you check out my blog at https://www.vivekiyyani. com/free. The beauty of articles is that I can always update them, and you even get to know the date of the last update. This is my invitation for you to join my newsletter where you get the latest updates to the information real-time and become a master at marketing to Millennials.

The Chapter I Struggled With

There's a chapter in this book that almost didn't make it in. It's a chapter that I didn't want to write because I felt I was giving away too much. It's an idea that has saved me a lot of time and made me quite fortunate. I'm usually pretty open about sharing ideas but I had to really mull over this before I decided to share it. I would hate for this idea to be devalued because it was given away so easily, despite having to work really hard to fully 'get it'. I hope you know which chapter I'm talking about. Sadly, you might have missed it and missed the gem without even realizing it. I'm not going to reveal which chapter it is. I'll leave it to you to discover and you can let me know if you found it by tagging me on Instagram @vivekiyyani, or by DM-ing me on LinkedIn. There is a slight chance that you might spot the chapter if you were to re-read the book. It's my hope and prayer that you spot this chapter, and leverage the knowledge in it and implement it as soon as possible. Don't let it slip away. This chapter will save you tons of time and earn you as much in income if you put the knowledge to good use. It's a bit like the Matrix—you will get to see things a lot more clearer once you get it. If you do get it, you will be on your way to more fun, freedom, and fortune in the near future. I wish you the best of luck!

To your success,
Vivek Iyyani

Scan QR code to get your bonus resources

Acknowledgements

This book wouldn't have been possible without the help and patience of many individuals. I am grateful to my wife Sushmitha for believing in me and my writing from the beginning. I have to thank her immensely for standing by me and pushing me to finish not just this book, but the other two before this as well. Writing 3 books back to back, while feeling burnt out, during the pandemic, is an enormous task. On top of that, being patient with an author is no small feat. Especially when writing a book takes so much time away from the family, even during the holidays. I'm very grateful to have a supportive and understanding spouse who held the fort while I worked on this book.

I would like to express my heartfelt gratitude to all the solopreneurs, entrepreneurs, business owners and marketers I've interviewed for this book. Thank you for your unwavering support and encouragement throughout this writing journey. Thanks to the Penguin team for their guidance and expertise in the publishing process which made this book a reality. Thank you for being patient with me. Lastly, a heartfelt thank you to all my readers and supporters for showing enthusiasm for my work and encouraging me to keep writing. This book would not have been possible without the love, support, and dedication of all those mentioned above. Your belief in me and this project means the world to me.

With deep appreciation,
Vivek Iyyani